Sri Garib Dass Oriental Series No. 165

MEMORY IN INDIAN EPISTEMOLOGY : ITS NATURE AND STATUS

Sri Garib Dass Oriental Series No. 165

MEMORY IN INDIAN EPISTEMOLOGY : ITS NATURE AND STATUS

Mrs. Shaila Bhandare

SRI SATGURU PUBLICATIONS
A division of
INDIAN BOOKS CENTRE
DELHI, INDIA

Published by :
Sri Satguru Publications
Indological and Oriental Publishers
A Division of
Indian Books Centre
40/5, Shakti Nagar,
Delhi-110007
(INDIA)

First Edition Delhi, 1993

ISBN-81-7030-359-1

Printed at :
D.K. Fine Art Press, Delhi.

PRINTED IN INDIA

To my parents,

LATE SMT. KAMALABAI V. DIGHE

AND

LATE SHRI VISWANATH S. DIGHE

who chose to realise their dreams of higher education through their children.

CONTENTS

PREFACE

This book is based upon my thesis for which I was awarded the degree of Ph.D. by the University of Bombay in January 1991. It is an attempt to establish on rational grounds what was always accepted as a matter of unanalysed conviction that it is impossible to treat memory as on par with dream-like illusory phenomenon and consequently to reject memory-cognition as invalid.

It was the inspiration and encouragement provided by Late Mrs. Taravahini Mudgal that prompted me to undertake this work in earnest—though the problem itself had attracted my attention for quite some time before. Dr. S.G. Mudgal, Additional Director, Ananthacarya Indological Research Institute (A.I.R.I.) has been my teacher and guide for about four decades and I consider myself singularly fortunate to have such an eminent indological scholar like him as my guide throughout my endeavour in research. No words will be sufficient to thank him for his persistent and genuine concern for his students and to appreciate his unusual gift of so guiding his students as to enable them to bring out the best in themselves.

I am also thankful to the Director, University Grants Commission for granting one year's study leave under faculty improvement programme and to the Principals of D.G. Ruparel College, Dr. B.R. Shinde and Shri A.P. Pradhan for recommending my candidature for this leave and for providing various facilities and concessions.

Thanks are also due to Dr. K.K.A. Venkatachari, Director, A.I.R.I., Bombay for his kind assistence in translating certain texts into English and also for allowing the free use of the Institute's library. I am equally indebted to Dr. B.N.K. Sharma, a renowned vedic scholar of international reput. In spite of his advanced age and consequent health problems, he readily spared some time for discussing certain problems from Dvaita epistemology and offered some new perspectives.

I thank my husband, Dr. V.V. Bhandare who has always encouraged me to aspire for the higher and higher goals of academic achievement and actively helped to reach them.

I am thankful to the Librarians and staff-members of the Libraries of D.G. Ruparel College, A.I.R.I., Bombay University, Fort and Jawahar Lal Nehru Library, Vidyanagari for making various required books available and extending other facilities.

Shri. Ramesh M. Joshi did an excellent job of typing in a very short span of time and in an absolutely flawless manner. Shri Sunil Gupta, of Indian Books Centre readily agreed to publish the book. The book in its published form speaks for the superb quality of printing and presentation. I sincerely thank both of them.

Mrs. Shaila Bhandare

Bombay

August, 1992

Chapter I

Introduction

Mṛtyuḥ sarvaharaścaham
Udbhavaśca bhavisyatām ।
Kīrtiḥ śrīrvakca nārīṇām
Smrtirmedhā dhrtiḥ kṣamā ।।

"I am death, the all-devouring and (am) the origin of things that are yet to be; and of feminine beings, (I am) fame, prosperity, speech, memory, intelligence, firmness and patience".[1]

In the tenth chapter of the Bhagavadgītā, the Lord is describing the divine manifestations or the divine glories by which He pervades all the worlds. These glories are the formative forces or spiritual powers where the Lord's presence is very clearly and prominently manifest. As such, these are also the fit objects for meditation. Among the feminine forms prominently displaying the divine excellence, MEMORY is one; this definitely emphasises the exalted status assigned to memory by the Lord Himself.

Naturally, when one turns to Nyāya, Mīmāmsā or Advaita Epistemology, one is intrigued to see the same memory being neglected, given cursory treatment, or criticised as being invalid knowledge. It is either treated as on par with hazy dreams and therefore incapable of giving valid knowledge or admitted as true but not valid. One wonders whether the Lord's declaration of smṛti as a 'vibhūti' is accidental and purposeless or the critics' analysis of memory is insufficient and in some cases even purposefully misleading. The present thesis has its origin in this dilemma and is an attempt to analyse and resolve it.

The importance of memory is not only for God as one of His divine manifestations in the feminine form, but it is also important for a devotee as one of the kinds of nine-fold devotion (navavidhā-bhakti) or rather one of the stages in the nine-fold devotion. Bhāgavata describes these nine stages as:

Śravaṅam kītanam viṣṇoḥ Smaraṇam Pādasevanam |
Arcanam vandanam Dāsyam Sakhyamātmanivedanam | |

—Listening to the praise of Viṣṇu (pertaining to His power, wisdom and goodness), praising Him, contemplating upon or remembering Him with a devout heart, serving Him, worshipping Him, bowing down before Him, doing all acts as His service, loving Him and totally dedicating oneself to Him—

Thus smaraṇa-bhakti or devotion at the stage of remembrance is nothing but incessantly meditating on the name, qualities, powers and sports of God and to be immersed in that meditation alone. Even Lord Kṛṣṇa, while directing Arjuna to the smaraṇa-bhakti tells him:

Ananyacetāḥ satatam yo mām smarati nityaśaḥ |
Tasyāham sulabhaḥ Pārtha nityayuktasya yoginaḥ | |

O Pārtha! Whoever with the feeling that there is none other than Me remembers Me ever continually, to that nitya-yukta, I am easy of attainment.

Even Nārada, while dividing devotion into eleven kinds of attachments (āsakti), admits smaraṇāsakti or attachment to proper remembrance as one important kind. It is passionate inclination to remembrance of God in all His magnificence.

In fact, remembrance plays so important a role in devotion that we cannot consider it as just one of the kinds or stages of devotion. It seems to pervade all stages of devotion. Even a moment's forgetfulness of God will be detrimental to the spirit of devotion. It is significant to note Rāmānujācārya's definition of meditation—Dhyāna—in terms of remembrance:

Dhyānam ca tailadhārāvat avicchinnasmṛtisantānarūpam |[2]

Meditation is of the nature of continuous and uninterrupted memory like the unbroken line of the flow of oil. This meditation which is of the nature of Smṛiti-santati is same as bhakti. The intense and uninterrupted contemplation and remembrance of God lead to the direct vision of God and eventually to His attainment. Attaining Him is reaching the stage of prapatti or 'dhruvānusmṛti' or the total surrender of one's being done in deep love for the Divine Being. This is the stage of sameness to God and of perpetual blissful existence. Bhakti or Smṛti-santati is no longer a means alone, but it becomes an end in itself. To love God is its own reward, to remember Him is an end in itself. To forget Him is to be caught and tossed up again in the whirlwind of the miseries of saṁsāra. That is the significance of the request made to God by Santa Tukarama:

Heci dāna degā devā | Tuza visara na vhāvā |
Guṇa gaīna āvaḍī! Heci māzī sarva joḍī | | [3]

"O God! Grant me only this favour that I shall never forget you." Memory of God has been the solace of our life; it is going to be our saving grace when it is time to cast off this bodily apparel, because only those who remember him at that last moment, come to the status of God's being, though such a remembrance is impossible to occur at the last moment if one has not cultivated it and steeped into it throughout one's lifetime. Such an assurance is given by Lord Kṛṣṇa to his devotees:

Anatakāle ca māmeva smaranmuktvā kalevaram |
Yaḥ prayāti sa madbhāvam yāti nāstyatra saṁśayaḥ | |

The importance of memory in devotion is thus undeniable and it is a memory of what one has seen, done, heard and read from authoritative sources. Can memory be still regarded as an invalid knowledge then? Or can we regard it as merely one of the many mental operations? The real problem pertaining to memory is its epistemological status.

In this context, an important point which has been instrumental in the suggestion of the problem of this thesis is the name 'Smṛti' given to the smṛti-literature. There are many who hold this literature in high esteem and next in importance only to the revealed texts. Viśiṣṭādvaita accepts it as equally authoritative and valid pramāṇa as the Śrutis. It is believed to be the very origin of the science of sacred duty. This is because the teachings contained in the smṛtis are believed to be based on Vedas and to provide the missing links in the vedas. Thus at times, a particular statement mentioned in a Smṛti text may not find a corresponding Śruti text in support of it. In such cases it is to be understood that the vedic text must have existed elsewhere at one time, and based on such texts, the statement has come down to us through the remembrance of the sages. It is quite in order to assume that the truths first came to the vedic sages as revealed or Śruta but the same were passed on by them to the subsequent generations and by these to the still next ones as revealed and remembered. At times the links were found missing, specially when the truths pertaining to the same topic were scattered in different Śrutis and were to be compiled together. These links were provided by the great sages through memory. Thus Smṛtis owe their origin to Śrutis and due to their freedom from deceit and delusions and due to deep knowledge of the world, society, duty, sacred law and punishment contained in them, they are treated on par with Śrutis. It is said that Vedas, the memory of vedic sages and their exemplary conduct form the roots of our science of righteous conduct.

It is obvious that outright denial of validity to memory will imply invalidity of smṛti- literature as well. We will be deprived of this great source of knowledge pertaining to the origin and nature of the universe, social organisations and obligations, righteous conduct, sacred law and compensation for the breach of its sanctity. Therefore it becomes imperative to examine the nature of memory and to see where its strength lies as a means of knowledge.

When we take a closer look at different sources of valid knowledge, we find each one making use of memory. Perception of an object for the first time or perception at its initial stage is vague sensation and does not yield any valid knowledge. It is only when sensation is followed by the remembrance of the interpretation of sensation that perception becomes a source of valid knowledge. Even a simple perceptual knowledge like, "This paper is white" is possible when we remember the concept of whiteness and that of paper and identify them in the present sense-data.

In recognition (Pratyabhijñā), memory of what was perceived in the past is as much important as what is being perceived in the present. The identity of the perceived object with the remembered one is the new knowledge we get through recognition.

Even inferential knowledge would be impossible without the aid of memory. Mere perception of smoke cannot lead to the new knowledge of fire unless one remembers the universal concomitance between smoke and fire, as in the case of kitchen.

The role of memory is even more obvious in comparison (Upamāna). Whether we interpret it as an instrument of knowledge of the denotative relation between a name of an unfamiliar object and the object itself or an instrument of knowledge of the resemblance of an unperceived object to the perceived one, the resulting knowledge would be impossible without memory. One ought to remember the object perceived in the past (cow) and also what the authoritative person has said about the object still unperceived then (gavaya).

Testimony (śabda) too makes extensive use of memory. Before we get the knowledge from the authoritative words or statements, we must recognise and remember the meaning signified by each word. Even the synthesis of the invididual meanings and the cognition of the meaning of the sentence as a whole depends upon memory.

Presumption (Arthāpatti) and Non-apprehension (Anupalabdhi) are not accepted by all as independent sources of valid knowledge. Leaving aside this controversy, one may ask—what is the importance of memory in them? Arthāpatti is an assumption of a fact which explains the fact to be accounted for. Whether we have to account for the perceived fact or the heard fact, the knowledge of the accounting or explaining fact can come from memory alone. The assumption which connects and explains the facts properly is a result of the synthesis of certain ideas from memory.

Non-apprehension is accepted by Bhāṭṭas and Advaitins as an independent source of valid knowledge. It is a means leading to the knowledge of the non-existence of a thing. Even this knowledge depends upon the memory of the knowledge of that thing when it was in existence. The non- cognition of a pot on the ground leads to the knowledge of the non-existence of a pot on the ground only when we have a recollective cognition of what is a pot, what it was like etc.

Memory is thus an important element in all the generally accepted pramāṇas. In other words, the discussion implies that memory is an important verificative instrument in all knowledges. Denying validity to memory will render all these pramāṇas suspect in authority and all knowledge as of doubtful origin.

This discussion is likely to imply that memory plays an auxiliary role in the attainment of knowledge as it is a faculty involved in all valid cognitions. But is it by itself a valid knowledge?

It may be pointed out in this context that our entire knowledge of the past is a memory-cognition. If memory-cognition is invalid, then our total knowledge of the past is invalid; it is not just the knowledge of the past, it is the knowledge of *our* past—the knowledge which is accompanied by the feelings of familiarity and strong belief. Moreover, through my remembrance I am aware that 'I' as the remembering being in the present is the same person as the perceiving being of the past. Thus, my recollections give me a kind of continuity, an assurance of my being the same person throughout. In short, my knowledge of personal identity is only through memory. Even our knowledge of the future is actually determined by our memory of the past. We believe that the future will be like the past we remember and of which we are sure. Our knowledge of causation is similarly rooted in memory. It is also impossible to account for our knowledge of duration without the help of memory. When we remember a thing, we also become aware of the time lapsed between its occurrence and its remembrance. The validity of memory-cognition assures the validity of all these cognitions. If we doubt the validity of memory, then not merely the valid knowledge of the past, but even that of the future becomes impossible. Our existence will be reduced to the very present moment in which we are living; there will neither be the solid past to rely upon nor the certain future to look forward to.

These results are too catastrophic to be accepted by any wise person. Hence it may be admitted that memory may be a kind of valid congnition. But it may still be insisted that it cannot be, a source or means of valid knowledge. (As it is, in Western philosophy, with the exception of the sceptics, there is generally no opposition to attributing validity to memory-cognition). But this will be a very queer stand to take. Here is a valid cognition which cannot be had through any one of the generally accepted means of valid knowledge. Memory itself has to be admitted as a special variety of perceptual process where one has a direct peep into the past, though at times it is also representational in nature, in which case, one looks into the past through the images. It is that variety of perception which cannot be reduced to any other variety and hence its independent status must be admitted.

This is the general outline of the course adopted in the development of the problem of this book. It has its origin in the conviction that memory cannot be rejected as invalid. It is true that various strong arguments are put forward against the validity of memory. Thus it is argued that memory-cognition is repetitive in nature and it does not give any new knowledge. In other words, its object is not unapprehended before. According to the Ńaiyāyikas, it is invalid simply because it is not a direct apprehension (anubhava) of an object. Śaṅkarācārya speaks of it as being of the nature of dreams which are distortions of reality and hence invalid. Similarly, it is held to be invalid because its object is no longer existing and hence the verification of knowledge is not possible. The most important argument against memory is that it is solely dependent upon earlier apprehension the validity or invalidity of which alone can decide the corresponding validity or invalidity of memory. According to the modern thinkers like Arvinda Sharma, the claim of memory to being a pramana must be accepted[4]; but Mr. G.P. Das, while criticising him maintains that memory cannot justify the knowledge-claims and hence cannot be a pramana.[5]

Such and a host of many other arguments are made against memory as a kind of knowledge and also as a method of knowledge. The arguments are powerful but not unanswerable and as such, they fail to shake the conviction that the invalidity of memory will leave the past unknown and the future unknowable.

There are equally strong and convincing arguments in favour of memory as a valid knowledge and a means of valid knowledge. We have already referred to some of them briefly. These as well as others are elaborated in the chapter on 'Status of Memory'. At present it should suffice to say that memory rejected as invalid knowledge will take away all other valid cognitions with it and an attempt to retain them can only succeed by including memory in them.

This analysis and discussion involves certain basic issues which also need to be laid bare. These issues are either philosophical or psychological in nature. We speak of memory as having epistemological status — of its being valid knowledge and also a method of valid knowledge. Starting with the basic concept of knowledge we note that there are many interrelated concepts that form the family of the concept of knowledge. Knowledge itself is the subject matter of Epistemology. Hence the need arises to analyse the concept of epistemology, its development in the West and in India, its relation to Metaphysics and Logic etc.

Even the concept of knowledge is in need of analysis because it is a well-known fact that knowledge is a very ambiguous word and admits of various senses. Even in philosophical discussions, it is variously understood as a substance, relation, activity and a property. Therefore, even before we try to establish that memory is a valid knowledge, we will be required to clarify different meanings and different status of knowledge and decide the sense and the status we ultimately accept.

The need to examine the concepts of pramā and pramāṇa is even more pressing. If we are not sure of what we mean by validity, it is practically impossible to decide whether memory is valid or not; in one sense of validity, it will be valid but not in another. Hence the detailed discussion pertaining to various accounts of what constitutes the validity of knowledge and methods of such knowledge, objections to some of them and finally fixing up the most acceptable sense or account is also in order.

In Western as well as Indian philosophy, the problem of memory is discussed in all its aspects. The Western philosophers have mainly discussed such problems as whether memory is presentational or representational in nature, whether images are indispensable or not, what are the kinds of memory, what are the essential functions of memory, if cognitive function is one of them etc.

The Indian philosophers too have discussed the nature of memory but have given more importance to the question regarding the validity or invalidity of memory-knowledge and also regarding memory being or not being a method of valid knowledge. They have defined memory with this specific aim before them. As we come to more and more recent thinkers, we find a general inclination to accept memory-knowledge as valid though a note of dissent is always to be found here and there. The spontaneity and certainty of memory, its being on par with apprehension (anubhava), its having exclusive access to certain knowledges are some of the notable features emphasised by the modern thinkers.

Whether memory can be valid knowledge or not and whether it can justify its claim to valid knowledge or not are philosophical questions to be asked about memory; but memory is also a psychological phenomenon and psychologists have shown interest in fathoming it. The nature and operation of memory, its corresponding counterparts in the cerebral make-up are some of the questions which primarily interest the psychologists. As they point out, memory is closely associated with thinking in general and learning in particular. Consequently, our full participation in life is made possible only by memory. The psychologists have rightly emphasised the close connection between perceiving and remembering. In fact, in their opinion, it is difficult to suggest a criterion which can clearly distinguish perceptions from recollections. This observation of the psychologists goes a long way in adding strength to our thesis that memory is a special kind of perception.

The psychologists have also noted that imagery makes very little difference to our recollections implying that memory is not always representative in nature. Their admission of the long-term memory speaks for the almost unlimited capacity of an individual to learn and to recall. This kind of memory is also marked for its organisation.

The most important contribution made by the psychologists to this problem is the continuity they have shown in the world of lower animals and that of humans so far as knowing from memory is concerned. The experiments have rendered the conclusion highly probable that even the lower animals can recall and know the past through memory. The dogs for example, can identify the objects through smell. The increased importance of memory in human knowledge becomes obvious and explicable. Hence it was thought reasonable to include a section on psychologists' views on memory.

This detailed discussion of the proofs, arguments and evidences for establishing that memory-knowledge is valid knowledge becomes necessary because the conviction that memory is both pramā and pramāṇa is not based upon blind faith in Smṛti as one of the feminine forms manifesting the divine excellence or in smaraṇa-bhakti (devotion through remembrance) offered by the devotees in order to reach the ideal of God-realisation or in smaraṇa-kṛpa, i.e. the favour of proper remembrance sought by the saints like Tukarama. The conviction is born of the rational arguments supported by the faith. To explain how this has happened is the subject matter of this book.

References

1. The Bhagavadgīta, edited by S. Radhakrishnan, p. 266.
2. R.B. I-1-1, p.17 quoted by S.M. Srinivasachari in Fundamentals of Viśiṣṭādvaita Vedanta, p. 284.

3. Abhanga 933, p. 204 — Sri Tukarama Maharajanchi Sartha Gatha.
4. Indian Philosophical Quarterly, Vol. X, No. 4, July 1983, p. 485.
5. Indian Philosophical Quarterly, Vol. XI, No. 1, January 1984, pp 131-135.

Chapter II

Epistemology

Epistemology in General and Indian Epistemology

"Epistemology, or the theory of knowledge, is that branch of philosophy which is concerned with the nature and scope of knowledge, its presuppositions and basis, and the general reliability of claims to knowledge"[1].

Man is essentially an epistemological creature. He finds himself in possession of various convictions or beliefs. These beliefs duly supported by the right to be sure constitute our knowledge. Man has an irrepressible urge to acquire knowledge; in fact this thirst for knowledge itself constitutes thesis about knowledge. But all convictions do not have the same value. Some are true, some are false. But the objective standards judging the validity of our convictions must be accepted as valid. A wholesale denial of the validity of all criteria is not possible. Absolute scepticism would put an end to all reasoned activity and will prove its own invalidity.

That some knowledge at least must be believed to be possible and valid is a thesis also insisted upon by Hegel. According to him the critique of epistemology cannot question the very existence and possibility of knowledge. Even as a critical inquiry concerning knowledge, epistemology must assume the existence of the faculty of cognition and its ability to yield valid results. In other instances it may be proper that, "we ought to become acquainted with the instrument, before we undertake the work for which it is employed. For if the instrument be insufficient all our troubles will be spent in vain" [2].

There is a traditional saying, viz. Mānādhīnā Meyasiddhiḥ, which means that the ascertainment of what is to be measured depends upon the measure itself. Applying this to the present problem, we get the result that the ascertainment of knowledge depends upon instrument of knowledge. But if we direct the instrument of cognition back upon itself, we are in fact examining knowledge through an act of knowledge which at least must be assumed to be and cannot be proved to be valid. To examine knowledge is to know it. Hence epistemology must begin with the assumption that there is knowledge. Even according to Russell, "some knowledge such as the knowledge of the existence of our sense-data, appears quite indubitable, however calmly and thoroughly we reflect upon it."[3]

This fact was recognised by Indian thinkers as well. Even Gautama, the author of Nyāya-Sūtras, has discussed this question whether it is possible to conceive the means of knowledge independently of knowledge and the objects of knowledge. According to him while the existence of the means of knowledge is proved by the fact that there is knowledge of objects, the validity of the means of knowledge is proved by themselves. The means of knowledge thus perform a two-fold function : they cause knowledge and also measure the validity of knowledge. In this respect they are like a lamp which illumines other things as well as itself.

It is therefore reasonable to believe that there are some things of which definite and valid knowledge is possible. Hence an investigation into the nature and means of knowledge is necessary. Epistemology is such a study which is a systematic reflection concerning knowledge. It takes knowledge itself as the object of science. Acquiring knowledge may be common to all men, but reflecting upon knowledge itself has been a concern of comparatively fewer thinkers.

It may be noted that epistemology is not concerned with particular epistemological statements like the life on the moon being improbable. It is rather concerned with such universal epistemological statements which can serve as standards in evaluating particular statements; for example, a statement like, "if a person remembers having had some experience before, he has reasonable ground to believe that it has occurred", or "someone's having an immediate experience of something is a sufficient reason for him to believe in the statement incorporating that experience", or "faults in the causal collocations are responsible for the errors in perceptual knowledge".

Various universal epistemological statements or rather, problems with which epistemology is concerned are : What is cognition as such ? What are its different forms? What is valid knowledge? What is the test of validity ? Why some forms of cognition are not accepted as valid?

These problems cannot be subsumed under logical or psychological problems. Epistemology has to be treated as a separate discipline. Still it is closely connected with Metaphysics, Psychology and Logic, though it is not always easy to ascertain the nature of this relation. It is really difficult to decide how, for example, epistemology is related to metaphysics, whether epistemology or metaphysics should precede the other; or perhaps none of them precedes the other; both are independent and yet supplementary to each other; because a particular theory of perception may be a result of a certain theory of the world or a theory of perception may give rise to a certain theory of the world. Perhaps we are only entitled to say that the epistemological theory of perception is logically related to the metaphysical theory of world.

It may be granted that epistemological problem is not the first for the human mind or for the race. Historically, Philosophy appears to begin with Metaphysics. The thinkers have raised the questions about the nature of the universe, its cause, the nature of reality. When the answers were difficult to arrive at or were found to be unsatisfactory that further inquiry into the nature of knowledge, its possibility etc. was found to be necessary.

The epistemological problems may also emerge as soon as men begin to reflect on knowledge itself. At the outset, knowledge is not a problem. We seem to take its nature and validity for granted. It is not concerned with itself : it is simple, immediate and direct, and carries the conviction that it is adequate and true. It is only when difficulties arise in the practical application of knowledge that the mind begins to reflect on knowledge, its origin, nature, processes, validity etc.

Whatever the origin of epistemological and metaphysical problems, these two disciplines, at least in part, are and should be independent. But in certain respects, they are interdependent. Epistemology, as dealing with the problems of logical reasoning, its constituents, validity, errors etc. can be investigated independently of Metaphysics. In fact, metaphysical reasoning has to abide by the rules of valid logical reasoning which can be known through epistemological criticism. But even here the ultimate postulates of thought must be justified by a system of metaphysics. It is true that the problems of immediate knowledge can be studied to a great extent independently of Metaphysics. But even here, the possibility of such a knowledge or the criticism of its value deserve metaphysical consideration.

On the whole, it seems fair to accept that epistemology and metaphysics are bipolar and inter-dependent. As Dr. P.B. Vidyarthi has pointed out 'While metaphysics without epistemology becomes dogmatic, epistemology without metaphysics lapses into nihilism and aggressive scepticism.[4]

In Indian Philosophy, metaphysics generally precedes epistemology. The nature of reality and the possibility of knowledge are ascertained on the grounds of revealing spiritual experiences. Epistemology only investigates different methods of knowledge and the problem of truth and error. Moreover, epistemology is subservient to metaphysics inasmuch as the Summum Bonum of life, the liberation, was considered to be attainable only through the true knowledge of the objects. The Buddhists differ in their priorities and revise metaphysics through the criticism of knowledge. But on the whole the tendency of the Indian thinkers seems to be to believe that the final guarantee of the epistemological theories would come from the truth of the metaphysical assumptions.

Epistemology and Logic

A similarly close relation exists between epistemology and logic. In fact epistemology can be distinguished from logic only if logic is treated in its purely formal aspect. Otherwise they appear to be substantially the same. Both systematic epistemology and systematic logic have taken their rise from the rules and forms of debating necessitated for producing conviction in others about the beliefs held by the thinkers.

It is the province of Logic to set forth the categories of mind, or the machinery by which it does its work. Epistemology accepts from Logic the deduction of the categories, their interrelations and their worth as instruments for the organization of knowledge.

It appears that in Indian Philosophy epistemology was always treated as a part of logic. While the works on epistemology confine themselves to a general treatment of the means of knowledge and the criterion of truth, those on logic undertake a detailed analysis and classification of the forms of knowledge and error, rules of definition and division, syllogistic reasoning, the classification of fallacies etc. Even in this respect, there is no hard and fast distinction and the practice varies greatly.

Epistemology and Psychology

Epistemology is also intimately connected with psychology, in so far as it has to depend upon an analysis of the mental processes which lead to various means of knowledge. The validity or invalidity of knowledge specially perceptual knowledge is determined respectively by the excellence or defects of causal factors, which include physical as well as psychological factors. Hence an enquiry into the nature of pramāṇas as well as erroneous experience has always been of a mixed nature—epistemological as well as psychological.

It is for this reason that some thinkers have called Epistemology, Psychology and Logic as mental sciences. Even Psychology deals with cognition but purely as a mental process. Epistemology accepts from the sister science of Psychology description of the process of knowing considered as an internal fact.

In a book like the present one the close connection between Epistemology and Psychology becomes even more obvious. In order to examine the claims of memory to be accepted as pramā and pramāṇa, it is necessary to acquaint oneself with the nature of memory as a mental event, its peculiarities and similarities with other cognitive processes like perception.

Indian Epistemology

In India, word epistemology never meant an enquiry into the possibility of knowledge which is variously called mathematical, scientific or metaphysical. It means an enquiry into the nature, kinds and sources of knowledge. The word 'Indian' merely conveys the specific geographical origin of this kind of epistemology.

Even Indian epistemology is primarily concerned with true knowledge or the problem of truth. It also exhaustively treats the problem of sources of knowledge and the nature of erroneous perception. But as N.V. Banerjee has pointed out the Indian epistemologists have generally failed to recognize the claim to truth borne by any given instance of knowledge and the actual truth or falsity of that knowledge. Consequently, what every source of valid knowledge furnishes is a truth-claim and not necessarily true or valid knowledge itself. In this light, then the distinction made between perception, inference, testimony, compartison on one hand and memory on the other appears arbitrary.

It is also to the credit of the Indian epistemologists that they are fully cognizant of the view that errors of perception are due to the defects of causal factors. But Indian epistemology goes further and analyses the contents of erroneous experience. Different schools of Indian philosophy have assigned a definite ontological status to the contents of erroneous experience.

Thus the problem of error figures as one of the main problems in Indian philosophy. What we believe to be an instance of a true cognition may really be an instance of error. But this really is a separate problem and not the problem of knowledge as such. Thus like any other cognition, if memory cognition turns out to be false, then it is a problem of error of memory-cognition and not of memory-cognition itself. Failing to realise this distinction the Western epistemologists have raised and tried to answer the fantastic problem of the possibility of knowledge. The Indian epistemologists on the other hand have enriched the field of epistemology by concerning themselves with the problem of error and by making serious attempt to solve it.

But the problem of truth and the problem of error are not the only concerns of Indian epistemology. As already mentioned cognition is produced by certain instrumental causes and it is essential for epistemology that it concerns itself with these instrumental causes or sources of knowledge. The Western philosophy is rather indifferent to this problem and does not deal with all the details of this problem as the Indian epistemology does.

But even here it is rather puzzling that these sources are called pramāṇas, implying thereby that they are the sources or instrumental causes of pramā, i.e. valid cognition. In reality they seem to be the instrumental causes of cognitions which may be true under some circumstances and false under others.

Most of the Indian thinkers accept the Vedas to be the origin of all kinds of knowledge. But it is evident that no epistemology as such can be found in the literature of the Vedic period. At the most it may be said that some verses in Ṛgveda are suggestive of the fact that perhaps Vedic seers were aware of the distinction between objects immediately present to and known through the senses and remote objects known through divine testimony or reflection. The Upaniṣads are credited with the distinction between knowledge and ignorance, i.e. vidyā and avidyā respectively, with the conception of self as the knower, the epistemological agent or subject that can never be the object and with the conception of the knowledge of the self forming the absolute knowledge which when attained results in the attainment of the knowledge of the entire universe.

The first systematic treatment of the problem of the means of knowledge is to be found in Gautama's Nyāya-Sūtras. It also deals with the objects of knowledge. The basic question for epistemology is—what is the nature of knowledge ? The next section examines various answers to this question and tries to determine which is the most acceptable account.

References

1. The Encyclopaedia of Philosophy, Volume 3, The MacMillan Company and the Free Press, New York, U.S.A. 1967, p. 8-9.
2. History of Indian Epistemology, Dr. Jwala Prasad, Introduction, p. 6.
3. Problems of Philosophy, Bertrand Russell, pp. 234-35.
4. Knowledge, Self and God in Ramanuja, p. 17, by Dr. P.B. Vidyarthi.

Chapter III

Problems Pertaining to Knowledge

Nature of Knowledge

Knowledge is generally speaking a set of convictions or beliefs a man possesses. Knowledge is preceded by the unsatisfactory state of mind in which one feels a curious uncertainty about something. Even according to Vātsyāyana, philosophical activity is something that is applied to objects, questions, problems or purposes about which we are uncertain or entertain a doubt. If we already know the answers, philosophical activity ends, and if we do not have any idea of the question itself, philosophical activity cannot begin. In short, knowledge is often arrived at through a certain process initiated by a doubt and sustained by inquiry. It is worth noting in this context that even this doubt contains as its essential component some knowledge in the minimal sense. The doubt and uncertainty are based upon some certainty or other. But the exact meaning of the concept of knowledge is not obvious and unitary. Philosophers in India as well as in the West—have envisaged the problem of knowledge, analysed it and tried to answer many relevant questions like: What is knowledge? What is the difference between valid and non-valid knowledge? What are the means of valid knowledge? etc.

It is true that this kind of epistemological inquiry is not the ultimate concern of Indian philosophers. Their true aim is liberation and the attainment of this highest state requires that we have true knowledge of the nature of objects, and of the highest state.

But it is also true that many philosophical controversies and difficulties arise due to insufficient analysis and understanding of the concept of knowledge and of the difference between different kinds of knowledge. The controversy regarding the status of memory as a source of knowledge in Indian philosophy is one such controversy. Hence the need arises for discussing and making precise the concept of knowledge.

As for the metaphysical nature of knowledge, it has been variously viewed, as an activity, a relation between certain entities, and a quality of the self.

Bauddha and Mīmāṃsā systems believe that knowledge is essentially of the nature of activity. It is an act of showing and leading to an object. Pārthasārathi emphatically remarks that knowledge is an act of the soul which produces a result in the object just as the act of cooking produces cookedness in the rice. While holding the view that knowledge is of the nature of activity, the behaviorists go to the extreme and believe that knowledge is a kind of behaviour, mere bodily activity.

Now, it has to be admitted that knowledge arises when the mind responds to stimuli from the surrounding world. Knowledge involves a process in which the mind actively reaches out to objects and illuminates them. It does involve activity and as such it is a dated event and a transient phenomenon.

But it is difficult to accept activity as the essential nature of knowledge. Jayant Bhaṭṭa has made various arguments against act-theory. According to him word 'knowledge' is derived from the verb 'to know' which denotes an activity. But all verbs need not denote activity. Moreover no activity of the soul is ever noticed.

It is indeed difficult to know the nature of activity involved in knowing; knowledge is the ground of activity but not identical with activity. 'Buddhi' and 'Karma' are distinct entities.

B.K. Matilal treats knowledge as a knowledge-episode[1] which in turn is a result of cognitive episode. The cognitive episode that has hit the truth is a knowledge episode according to him. He admits that knowing does not mean being in a special state of mind but still insists that knowing seems to be always derived from some cognitive episode or occurrence.

He holds further that the episodic nature of knowledge does not imply that as soon as the moment is over and the occurrence is gone, knowledge too would be gone forever. Knowledge does not run away even when the perceptual event is over.

Knowledge or knowing episode is the culmination or end-product of a perceptual process.

He makes a very careful distinction between acts and episodes and defends the use of 'knowledge episodes'. 'Acting' according to him primarily applies to physical movement and observable physiological behaviour. Moreover 'act' has certain other implications as well; it needs an object which is acted upon, an actor or agent, primarily a conscious and animate body. In comparison, the demands of episode on our imagination are minimal. Each episode is an effect but is not necessarily an act. Episode can be looked upon as happening or occurring but not necessarily as 'acting'.

Many realists believe knowledge to be a kind of relation between certain elements. Thus according to the critical realists, knowledge is a relation between the mind, the object and the datum or the character-complex. The realists like C.D. Broad and G.E. Moore accept knowledge as a relation between mind and object. Even Russell accepts it as a kind of relation. According to the American neo-realists, knowledge is a relation between ojbects and not between a subject and an object.

But to be is not to be related. Knowledge may be admitted to arise out of the soul's relation with the body. But it is a new phenomenon and not itself of the nature of relation. Even a relation is a cognitum or an object of relation. Moreover if knowledge is a relation, a question would arise: How do we know knowledge?

Advaita Vedānta View

According to Advaita Vedānta right knowledge is transcendental in nature and the entire field of empirical knowledge is wrapped in the veil of ignorance. Nescience is the cause of all empirical distinctions of knower, known and knowledge. The instruments of knowledge, the knowledge itself and the empirical ego that knows are all relegated to the domain of nescience. The real nature of things is not known to us. The so-called knowledge is a distortion rather than revelation of the real. Hence knowledge can have at best only a pragmatic status having no theoretical significance and validity at all.

All distinctions (knower, known and means) follow the superimposition of the not-self on the self. In a cognitive act, the nescience-generated internal organ goes out through the channel of the eyes etc., pervades the object and takes its form which is called vṛtti or modification. This modification of ego reflecting itself in consciousness gives rise to knowledge. The knowledge thus becomes the attribute of ego and not that of the self. It is the function of vṛtti to manifest objects. The vṛtti forges a connection between the self (caitanya) conditioned by the object and the knowing self.

Where there is no operation of the internal organ, and there is still cognition, it is the internal organ that has transformed itself into a vṛtti and is manifested by witness-consciousness.

Thus without ignorance, knowledge cannot be a fact. Therefore, all knowledge – the operation of all means of cognition and objects of cognition, secular or spiritual and all the sāstras have for their presupposition, superimposition or ignorance.

According to the Naiyāyikas, Mādhvas and Jaiṇas, knowledge is of the nature of quality of soul. According to Nyāya school, knowledge cannot be a substance because it is not the constitutive cause of anything. The different words such as Buddhi, Upalabdhi, Jñāna and Pratyaya have exactly the same meaning. Knowledge includes all congnitions which have more or less determinate objective reference. It is a property of manifestation or illumination of objects. It is a property which is the ground of our behaviour because our dealings with objects are determined by our knowledge of them. It is not a physịcal quality observable by the external senses. It is not even an essential property of the soul but only acquired by it in its bodily setting. In other words, it is an adventitious attribute of selves. A queer result which follows from such an account of knowledge is that when self is bereft of knowledge, self is reduced to insentient entity.

Knowledge by its nature is without any form; whatever peculiar definite form it acquires is due to object itself (Arthenaiva viśeṣo hi nirākāratayā dhiyām — Udayana—Kusumāñjali).

Lastly, Nyāya school understands knowledge in a broad sense to stand for any awareness whatsoever. Hence first it is classified into presentative and representative and presentative knowledge is further classified into true and false.

Jaina View

Even according to Jainas Cetanā or consciousness is the very defining characteristic of the soul. Strictly speaking, soul is a substance which possesses four infinites: infinite intuition, infinite knowledge, infinite bliss and infinite power. The liberated souls possess all these infinites; the worldly Jīvas do not possess them in all their perfection.

Jainas make the distinction between Darśana and Jñāna or intuition and knowledge. Intuition or darśana is a kind of preliminary step to or initiation into knowledge or jñāna. Darśana is a stage of simple awareness of an object or the awareness of its existence (sattāmātra) or its belonging to class but the details are not perceived.

Jñāna corresponds to the determinate phase in the process of getting knowledge. The sense awareness of the apprehension state is converted into sense-perception. The passage from darśana to jñāna is from the raw unverbalised stage in acquiring knowledge to a stage in which language can be employed to clearly indicate various elements in the knowledge.

Viśiṣṭādvaita View

Even Rāmānuja treats the problem of knowledge as central and integral to his philosophy. Knowledge is both a substance and a quality according to him. It is a substance as it constitutes the essence of selves and God; it is also a quality of God and souls. The self owns knowledge. Through his attributive knowledge of dharmabhūta jñāna, self comes into contact with the object and gives rise to what we call knowledge. It thus illumines the object and itself too. Knowledge is what the subject has for its experience. It is not itself knowledge.

Knowledge, according to Rāmānuja presupposes synthesis of subject and object. To know is to know an object. Human knowledge cannot be what it is without an object external to it.

But knowledge is also equally inconceivable without a subject. Knowledge illumines the object. It is an essential function of the subject. In fact it is the product of the mutual relation of both the subject and the object; it is a matter of relational consciousness.

This discussion does not imply that there is no knowledge without an empirical object. Rāmānuja thinks that knowledge is *eternal* although its manifestation takes place when it illumines an object. Thus even in deep sleep or unconsciousness, when there is no illumination of objects, knowledge is still there. It illumines the subject instead of the object. There is always the subsequent awareness of the experience of deep sleep or unconsciousness as the case may be, and this awareness comes through reminiscence.

This shows that knowledge not only reveals an object but also reveals itself to its substratum, i.e. soul. If knowledge cannot reveal itself as an object, then past knowledge and the knowledge or experience of another mind will be impossible.

Thus, whatever the source from which knowledge is derived, it is always relational and has for its contents only objects with qualities. A theoretical distinction between a 'that' and a 'what' of an object can be made; but the object itself must be a 'that-what'.

Lastly, Rāmānuja maintains that no knowledge is representative. Knowledge must be presentative. This is implied by the concept of knowledge as a matter of relational consciousness or a matter of subject- object synthesis.

Knowledge is also taken to be fluid or dynamic in character. As a result it flows out to the object directly. According to Viśiṣṭādvaita, jñāna, the attributive intelligence of the self starts from the ātman and with manas and indriyas comes into contact with the object, assumes its form and reveals it. The knowledge of the object thus arises when jñāna contacts the object through the inner and outer sense-organs.

The concept of dharma-dhūta jñāna or attributive knowledge is the foundational truth of the Viśiṣṭādvaita theory of knowledge. Jñāna is an attribute of self; they are separate but not separable. Being and 'knowing' cannot be identical nor can they be entirely unrelated. So what 'is' or 'exists' must have a quality and quality must have substance as its ground. Atman is substantive intelligence and attributive intelligence as well. The attributive intelligence or dharmabhūta-jñāna is self-illumined and it also illumines objects. But it is only revelatory and is not self-realized. It is like physical light which can show but cannot know. The self alone is a knowing subject. All states of consciousness are modifications or avasthās of this jñāna. It is the same consciousness which persists in dreamless sleep, swoon and even liberation.

Dvaita View

Dvaita school of Madhvācārya advocates realistic epistemology. The objects of knowledge exist independently of the knowing mind. Moreover, the objects known necessarily possess attributes. It is the knowledge that is determined by objects; the form of knowledge is determined by the attributes of objects, hence knowledge is always determinate in nature.

The object and its knowledge are connected through a very peculiar relation which is called viśaya- viśayī-bhāva or the relation between the revealed and the revealer. This relation is not a part of knowledge but is external to it. For each object there is a separate viśaya-viśayī-bhāva to connect it with its own separate cognition.

The subject of knowledge is self. Knowledge is an eternal property of soul. Thus knowledge is essentially attributive in nature. It belongs to the self and is yet different from the self. Dvaita school of Madhva rejects the contention of Advaita Vedānta that self and knowledge are identical. They also reject the Naiyāyika contention that knowledge is an adventitious property of soul or something which belongs to the soul in its embodied state, because in that case, when bereft of knowledge the soul would be reduced to an insentient entity. Knowledge is a unique relational property of the self whereby self as a subject or knower gets related to its object under specific conditions.

The self is the agent that initiates the knowing process in which manas is the chief instrument. The manas undergoes transformation according to the qualities of the object. This transformation is the knowledge of the object. Thus the knowledge possessed by individual souls is always vṛtti-jñāna or knowledge of modifications.

Taking into consideration various metaphysical views on the nature of knowledge, we find that the theory that the knowledge is of the nature of quality is more commonly accepted than any other. Even admitting the episodic nature of knowledge, the essential nature of the result of knowledge-episode is a quality which illuminates the nature of object. It is argued that a quality does not point to anything beyond, while as reference to objects is inherent in the very nature of knowledge. To this it may be replied that knowledge is a relational property and as such reference to the object is inevitable.

In its empirical nature knowledge is awareness or apprehension of objects. Awarcness is knowledge in its simplest form. The nature of knowledge as awareness implies the duality between the mind which is aware and the object of which it is aware. This object may be a thing, a quality, a mental state, a physical entity etc. Empirically, knowledge is also the ground of all intelligent activity[2]. Our dealings with other objects are determined on the basis of some knowledge. We have desires, aversions, efforts for objects and we find objects to be pleasant or painful because of the knowledge of objects. As an apprehension of objects, knowledge includes many cognitive states like perception, inference, comparison, memory, doubt, dreams, illusions etc.

From the logical point of view, many characteristics of knowledge are mentioned which limit the scope of its application. Many Western thinkers like Stebbing, Russell, Ayer insist that true cognition alone is knowledge. Thus it must be an assured cognition (as distinct from doubt). But knowledge does not merely mean subjective certainty. It must also be a true cognition of objects. In other words, it must represent its object with that nature and character which really belong to it. To these characteristics, Naiyāyikas also add presentational nature (anubhava) as an important characteristic of knowledge. Mīmāṁsakas mention another characteristic of knowledge as logically understood. For them, knowledge must be a new cognition. The objects already known do not need to be known again. Knowledge must add new contents to the mind and thus must have original character.

As a conclusion of this discussion, we may say that knowledge is empirically any awareness of an object which forms the basis of all our intelligent activity, specially of the difference in activity in respect of different objects. In its narrow logical sense, it may be treated as an assured true cognition. But it is difficult to see and maintain why knowledge in its logical nature must be either presentational or novel. Its fundamental or in-itself nature is neither substance, nor activity nor relation; it is quality which manifests objects to us.

CONCEPT OF VALIDITY

Prāmāṇya or Validity

Discussion regarding the nature of knowledge leads one to the problem of truth of knowledge. Knowledge understood in its broad sense includes all kinds of cognition irrespective of the question of truth and falsehood. The thinkers like N.V. Banerjee choose to employ the word cognition in this broad sense, i.e. as corresponding to jñāna and the word knowledge in the sense of true cognition, i.e. pramā. Every cognition, according to him, bears claim to truth but only some cognitions are true while some others are false. What is common to true and false cognitions? Both attempt to manifest the object with its general characters. But true cognition has certain characteristics which distinguish it from apramā or mithyā-jñāna, i.e. false cognition.

An inquiry into these characteristics or nature and criterion of truth has received a well-deserved treatment both in the Indian as well as Western epistemology. Like their Western counterpart, Indian philosophers have expressed divergent views on the meaning of truth, though all of them are unanimous that truth is the distinguishing mark of pramā. These divergent views may be summarised as follows:

The *Nyāya* works regard truth as the faithfulness with which knowledge reveals its object. According to Jayanta, pramā is that knowledge of object which is free from doubt and error. (vyabhicāriṇīmasandigdhāmarthopalabdhīm vidadhati I)[3]

According to Gaṅgeśa pramā is the apprehension of the existence of something in a place where it really exists. (Yatra yadasti tatra tasyānubhavaḥ I)[4] A similar account of truth has been given by Annam Bhaṭṭa. According to him true cognition is apprehension of an object having an attribute as possessing that attribute. (Tadvati tatprakārakaḥ anubhavaḥ yathārthaḥ I sa eva prametyucyate I)[5]

Such a definition of truth refers to two aspects which are equally important. Truth is basically a property of knowledge and not of the object. Thus it refers to an epistemological situation — knowledge having a certain qualifier. But it also refers to an ontological situation — the fact that the qualifier of knowledge really belongs to the object of knowledge. It is then a relational property which at once refers to both the object and the knowledge. Thus truth is no doubt a unitary concept having heterogeneous components.

It may be noted that the Naiyāyikas divide cognition into memory and apprehension and state that memory-cognition itself may be true or false depending upon whether it correctly reveals the past apprehension or fails to do so. Still memory as such is accepted as non-valid knowledge as it is not apprehension (anubhava) and only apprehension can be a valid knowledge as it alone can arise out of objects themselves.

According to the Vijñānavāda Buddhists, true cognition is practically useful knowledge. It reveals an object that serves some purpose or leads to the achievement of some end. In still other words, it is that which favours a successful volition.

The Prābhākaras believe that on the cognitive side all knowledge is true. On the practical side, some knowledge is said to be false when it leads to unsuccessful behaviour. This is perhaps understanding truth in its broadest sense as applicable to all awareness. It is co-extensive with the property of being an awareness of or being true to the object.

Kumārila himself does not give any precise definition of truth. But a line — Bodhātmakatvena svataḥprāptā pramāṇatā[6]—suggests that even for him truth is same as awareness of the object (Bodhātmakatva). Gāgābhaṭṭa defines true knowledge as a knowledge whose object was previously unknown and which is uncontradicted by another knowledge. (Ajñātaviṣayakatvam bādhakajñānarahitajñānam pramā — Bhāṭṭacintāmaṇi, p. 13)[7] Bhāṭṭas have thus suggested two notions of truth:

(i) truth as nothing other than awareness of the object, and
(ii) truth as involving novelty and uncontradictedness.

Advaita Vedānta View

As per the Advaita Vedānta account, empirical knowledge is consciousness as limited by the modification of the inner sense. The valid means of knowledge reveal their objects as the Sun or a lamp would manifest the things, both beautiful and ugly alike. Knowledge is valid when it has for its content an entity not already known, and is not sublated. Thus truth is explained by Dharmarāja in terms of novelty or originality (anadhigatatva) and uncontradictedness (abādhitatva). Rāmadvaya defines right knowledge as that which presents the object as it is. This definition gives more realistic basis to knowledge. Even novelty is not acceptable to Rāmadvaya as a criterion of validity. Gauḍabrahmānandi suggests that truth is the property of being the knowledge of anything which has not been known to be false. Thus every knowledge is true so long as its erroneous character is not detected. Madhusūdana insists that truth is the property of being a certain apprehension of an object which was previously unknown. (Ajñātārthaniścayātmakatvameva prāmāṇyamasmatpakṣe — Advaitaratnarakṣaṇam)[8]. Śrī Harṣa in his Khaṇḍanakhaṇḍakhādya argues against the criterion of unsublatability on the ground that even a wrong cognition may not be sublated by any other cognition. It is possible that a faulty perception may be contradicted by any other faulty perception; even a right perception may be sublated by a subsequent erroneous perception. If it is insisted that a contradiction can be only by a faultless perception we are arguing in a circle; the reason is that we cannot say at any time what is a faultless perception without some reference to the fact of contradiction.

According to Citsukha, commentator on Śrī Harṣa's work, it is not possible to say whether any piece of knowledge will continue to remain uncontradicted for all time.

Generally Bhāṭṭas have considered novelty or originality as an essential part of the truth which is the differentiam of knowledge. The real reason for giving so much importance to the character of novelty is to deny the status of knowledge to memory which does not give us the knowledge of 'new' but only reminds us of what we already know. If mere uncontradictedness is believed to be the essence of truth, then the status of knowledge will have to be assigned to memory as well because it may be uncontradicted or undoubted. It may be noted in this context that while novelty or anadhigatatva is introduced in the concept of validity in order to exclude memory, uncontradictedness or non-sublatability is common to both kinds of definition of validity—that which includes and that which excludes memory.

But the concept of novelty as constituting the essence of truth is beset with many difficulties some of which are brought to our attention by Jayant. Jayant does not accept that knowledge which refers to the previously known objects is invalid. Memory is still not valid knowledge, even according to him, but it is so because its object is non-existent at the time of remembrance.

If novelty is the essence of truth, what is the status of the persistent knowledge of the same object? Is it still true at the subsequent moments also? It is so according to all thinkers though they have given different reasons for accepting it as true. Some thinkers believe that it is not at all the same object at the subsequent moments. It is an object which has changed its temporal aspect and thus renders novelty to the knowledge.

But different movements are not really perceived as different because they are too small to be noted as different. And still the knowledge of subsequent moments is valid because the subsequent knowledge is not solely determined by the knowledge of the previous moment. It is caused by the very objective conditions which cause the knowledge of the previous moment. However, on this view it is difficult to see how knowledge can have novelty, if it is the same object and the same objective conditions determining knowledge. The Advaitins believe that the knowledge does not change from moment to moment and it persists so long as fresh knowledge does not replace it.

Dvaita:

According to Madhvācārya, truth is the capacity of knowledge to reveal the nature of an object as it really is: Yathāvasthitajñeyaviṣayīkāritvam[9] (Pramāṇa Lakṣaṇa). True knowledge does not go beyond artha, i.e. the knowable object. Jayatīrtha defines true knowledge as the knowledge of a thing as it actually is, with reference to a particular space-time setting; (Yathāvasthitameva jñeyam viṣayīkaroti, nānyathā!)

The knowledge must answer to the nature of an object. But correspondence here does not mean exact spatio-temporal co-existence between knowledge and its object. It is not expected to be complete correspondence of knowledge with all aspects of the object. Truth means the existence of such aspects in the knowledge as are actually perceived by each person according to the extent of his capacity or understanding and other conditions governing the rapprochement to the object.

Viśiṣṭādvaita:

Viśiṣṭādvaita accepts that jñāna is self-valid and true, that the sat or real alone is cognised and that there is no knowledge of asat or unreal. Through his analysis of the concepts of truth and error, Rāmānuja argues that all knowledge is real having in all its forms an objective basis, and that we never perceive what is not given and that at no level of our experience are we ever confronted with mere illusions.

Valid knowledge is defined by Venkatanātha as: Yathāvasthitavyavahārānuguṇam jñanam prameti![10]. Knowledge which corresponds to or produces a behaviour leading to an experience of things as they are. The definition includes behaviour as an indispensable condition of pramāṇa. It is possible that in a particular case a behaviour may not be actually induced; it may yet be pramāṇa if the knowledge be such that it has the capacity of producing a behaviour which would tally with things as they are.

Thus truth is not merely the knowledge of an object as it is but also what conduces to practical behaviour. The definition of truth thus combines the realist and the pragmatic elements, or the theoretical and the practical aspects of knowledge. Thus knowledge is true not only when it refers to the character of the object but when it meets with the expected result.

Truth, accordingly does not concern merely the sensory apprehension of an object but also the successful activity or causal efficiency. Thus, every kind of knowledge is true if it is consistent with experience in its exactitude. In fact this is what distinguishes truth from error which is also presentative and real as it too has objective basis.

Truth, then must be self-consistent and proof of its own being. It must at once exhibit its own inner consistency and self-validity. As Dr. K.C. Varadachari puts it, ". . . even as the Buddhists, Jainas and pragmatists claim, the nature of truth is dynamic and every truth exhibits purposiveness which need not be specially that which pleases us or any one"[11].

Meghanādāri defines pramāṇa as the knowledge that determines the objects without depending on other sources of knowledge such as memory. Thus, measuring the nature of object is essential feature of valid knowledge. Meghanādāri's definition, then gives importance to the function of valid knowledge, and not to its correspondence or its tendency to result in a certain behaviour.

The discussion of the problem of validity makes us aware of a number of features assumed to belong to it. It is variously regarded as faithfulness with which cognition reveals its object, apprehension of object free from doubt and error; experience or apprehension which represents the object as it actually is; practical usefulness; novelty; uncontradictedness; correspondence; capacity to initiate behaviour which results in the experience of object as it really is, being independent of other pramāṇas etc.

The entire discussion ultimately has bearing upon the vital problem of this book: status of memory in Indian Philosophy as a source of valid knowledge. The concept of validity is interpreted in various ways — some of the interpretations aim at only excluding memory from the kinds and instruments of valid knowledge and thus they serve only a negative function. Among these may be mentioned novelty, being of the nature of experience or apprehension, not depending upon other sources of knowledge etc.

Other interpretations of validity mention such features which belong both to apprehension and memory. Being practically useful, having capacity to reveal the object as it really is, having capacity to produce successful activity, uncontradictedness, having agreement with knowledge in others' minds, vividity, spontaneity, steadiness are such features which belong to both apprehension and memory.

It is also interesting to note that certain features are fundamental to the concept of validity, while as certain other features are secondary to it, in the sense that valid knowledge generally has these features but they are rather the consequences of, and not the essence of validity. Yāthārthya i.e. the capacity of knowledge to reveal the nature of an object as it really is, is the most and the only fundamental feature of validity. The knowledge which does not have it will not be valid knowledge. In other words, yāthārthya and pramātva (i.e. being true to the nature of object and being valid) are the same. An attempt to treat them as separate (and thus to treat memory as true but not valid) is not only arbitrary but also smacks of some ulterior motive. But this is exactly what the Naiyāyikas have done.

Other features of validity, in comparison to yāthārthya, are of secondary importance. Knowledge is first valid and therefore it is practically useful, or results in the behaviour which gives us experience tallying with the nature of object or is uncontradicted or is steady or vivid. These features do belong to valid knowledge but it is difficult to say that they constitute validity.

Moreover, some of these features may or may not belong to valid knowledge and when they do not, it does not affect their validity. Thus every valid knowledge may not result in any activity, or may not be equally vivid or may not correspond with the knowledge of others or at times even valid knowledge may be contradicted by subsequent invalid knowledge.

It, therefore, is the most satisfactory explanation of validity that it is nothing but yāthārthya or the knowledge of a thing as it actually is or as it answers the nature of a thing. The valid knowledge must include the existence of such aspects as actually belong to and are actually perceived by the person. It is obvious that the persons differ according to their capacities and hence their understanding of the same object may not be same. Even the conditions pertaining to space and time governing our cognition are not same. The word, 'yathā' in yāthārthya refers to the existence of all such aspects as actually belong to and are actually cognised by the person according to his capacities and other conditions of space and time. Such an account of validity would not be too rigorous to exclude some forms of valid knowledge nor too flexible to include doubt and error which are obviously instances of invalid cognition.

The discussion of the concept of validity naturally raises the question: Which are the sourcer or instruments of valid knowledge generally accepted by Indian philosophers? This is the problem we shall discuss in the next section.

Concept of Pramāṇas, i.e. Means of Valid Knowledge

Any theory is an answer or a set of answers to a question or a set of questions. This statement is true of theory of knowledge as well. We have already discussed some of the questions like: What is knowledge? What is the distinction between valid and invalid knowledge? What is meant by validity?

One more question which is equally important is: What are the methods of arriving at valid knowledge? Knowledge in general is analysable into ideas. It is true that ideas constitute knowledge when they have been systematised and absorbed by the knowledge. But it is also to be noted that all our ideas are not true. Hence the inquiry into the origin and validity of all knowledge is in order. In order to analyse how the knower knows the known, the analysis and understanding of the means of knowledge is necessary. It is not sufficient to ascertain what is knowledge and what is truth but we must also ascertain the means which give true knowledge.

Indian Logic deals mainly with the problems concerning the means and methods of acquiring, ascertaining and analysing knowledge. It is believed to be a remarkable feature of Indian Epistemology that it has thought it fit to deal with the problem of the sources of valid cognition. In the words of Max Müller, "Such an examination of the authorities of human knowledge ought, of course to form introduction to any system of philosophy. To have clearly seen this is, it seems to me, a very high distinction of Indian philosophy. . . .Supported by these inquiries into the evidences of truth, the Hindu philosophers have built up their various systems of philosophy or their various conceptions of the world, telling us what they take for granted and then advancing step by step from the foundation to the highest pinnacles of their system."[12]

But an observation made by Nikunja Bihari Banerjee is important in this connection. According to him the distinction between cognition and knowledge corresponds to the distinction between jñāna and pramā. In this sense knowledge presupposes cognition inasmuch as it is a final point in a process in which cognition is its immediate precedent. The cognition itself is due to certain preceding conditions regarded as its occasional cause; it is also open to the distinction between truth and falsity. These considerations lead to the question regarding its source or sources. This question is very essential to epistemology and various schools of Indian philosophy have taken keen interest in this problem.

But he also notes in this connection that the sources of cognition are called pramāṇas which implies that these are instrumental to pramā (or yathārtha-jñāna or true cognition) instead of mere cognition which is open to the distinction of truth and falsity. Hence, according to him it is evident that Indian philosophy has, at least by implication missed the truth that the sources concerned yield cognition or jñāna which may prove to be pramā in one set of circumstances or apramā in another.

The sources also determine the peculiar features of the knowledge we obtain. The knowledge from sense experience has a kind of directness and immediacy which is lacking in inferential knowledge. The inferential knowledge, on the other hand is marked by necessity and fixedness which are due to the knowledge of universality as yielded by vyāpti. If memory is admitted as a source of valid cognition (as is attempted thro' these pages) the knowledge arising out of it will have to be accepted as having the same immediacy and directness as belong to perceptual knowledge, though not perhaps the same kind of verifiability.

As regards the problem of the sources of cognition, Indian philosophy displays two opposite tendencies towards its solution. On one hand, we have Cārvākas who are unduly strict and rigorous in their consideration of means of cognition. They accept only perception (pratyakṣa) as a source of valid cognition. Later Cārvākas like Purandara accept inference only in respect of empirical knowledge. This is like the Positivists who started with Direct Verification and ended up admitting Indirect Verification too. In comparison to Cārvākas, Paurāṇikas appear to be over-indulgent when they accept perception (pratyakṣa), inference (anumāna), testimony (śabda), comparison (upamāna), Presumption (arthāpatti), non-apprehension (anupalabdhi), inclusion (sambhava) and tradition (aitihya). Thus they display the other opposite tendency by indiscriminately inflating the sources. Vaiśeṣikas and Bauddhas accept only perception and inference. In the hands of Sāṃkhya-Yoga schools the number increases to three due to the addition of testimony. Nyāya school adds comparison to these three. Pramāṇas acceptable to Prābhākaras are perception, inference, testimony, comparison and presumption. According to Bhāṭṭa and some Vedānta schools valid cognition can be obtained from perception, inference, testimony, comparison, presumption and non-apprehension. Mention has been made in Indian philosophical literature of two more sources of cognition respectively called gesture (ceṣtā) and elimination (pariśeṣa).

If we are to decide whether these sources are genuine and independent or not, we have to deal with them separately. But even prior to that, an analysis of the concept of pramāṇa is necessary in order to determine that all sources of valid cognition are taken into account and none satisfying the criterion of pramāṇa is omitted — either inadvertently or through insufficient analysis or through failure to correctly apply the analysed concept.

What is prāmāṇa

The term 'pramāṇa' consists of the root 'mā' with a prefix 'pra' and suffix 'lyut'. It is used in two senses (1) true knowledge and (2) the means or instruments giving rise to it, according to the two senses of the suffix "ana" (lyut), (Bhāve 'lyuṭ' and karaṇe 'lyuṭ') Madhvācārya distinguishes these two senses and usages of the term and coins two separate terms 'kevala' and 'anu' pramāṇa to denote them.

The word 'pramāṇa' is generally used in the second sense, i.e. anupramāṇa or means of valid knowledge. There is, however, a marked difference of opinion regarding the exact meaning and nature of pramāṇa understood even as 'means of knowledge' amongst the philosophers.

> Avisaṁvādi vijñānam pramāṇamiti saugatāḥ।
> Anubhūtiḥ pramāṇam sā smṛteranyeti kecana।
> Ajñātacaratattvārthaniścayakamathāpare।
> Prameyavyāptamapare pramāṇamiti manvate।
> Pramāniyatasāmagrīm pramāṇam kecidūcire। —
> Tārkikarakṣā by Varadarāja[13].

According to the Buddhists, pramāṇa is knowledge which has identity of content between the cognition and cognitum; some say that it is apprehension which is other than memory; still others maintain that it is that which determines the essential nature of previously unknown object; some believe that it is what is extensive with object of knowledge and some say that it is a collocation of conditions producing valid knowledge.

It is worth our while to examine some of the important views on 'pramāṇa'.

According to Kaṇāda, the general definition of pramāṇa should be based upon the principle that the cause of cognition should be free from defects. Śrīdhara refers to an additional characteristic 'adhyavyavasāya' meaning that vidyā is a definite cognition. Śaṅkara Miśra in his 'upaskāra' on the Vaiśeṣikasūtra asserts that a pramāṇa is that which produces true knowledge.

Coming to the Nyāya Views on pramāna, we note that Gautama enumerates four pramāṇas but does not explain the term pramāṇa itself. According to Vātsyāyana, pramāṇa is that which causes cognition or which is the instrument of valid knowledge. The means of knowledge have a necessary reference to an object (for it is only when objects are cognised through means of knowledge that it is possible to make an effort to acquire them). The credit for giving a really comprehensive Nyāya definition of pramāṇa goes to Jayant. According to him, pramāṇa is that collocation of conscious as well as unconscious factors which results in producing such an apprehension of knowable objects that is different from illusion and doubt. (Avyabhiçāriṇīmasandigdhāmarthopalabdhim vidadhatī bodhābodhasvabhāvā samagrī pramāṇam! Bodhābodhasvabhāvā hi tasya svarūpam, avyabhicārādi viśesaṇārthopalabdhisādhanatvam lakṣaṇam I)[14].

Thus distinctive feature of an instrument of knowledge lies in the fact that its presence is invariably followed by the knowledge of an object and this feature belongs only to the aggregate of conditions.

According to him, pramāṇa is a collocation which is different from a subject and an object —

> Tasmāt kartṛkarmavilakṣaṇā saṁśaya—
> viparyayarahitārthabodhavidhāyinī bodhābodhas-
> vabhāva samagrī pramāṇamiti uktam![15].

The other features are the same as noted above.

The characteristic 'Bodhābodhasvabhāva' suggests that collocation of conditions constituting pramāṇa includes consciousness as well as unconscious objects. In fact, consciousness is a result of pramāṇa and not itself a pramāṇa. At the most it may be an indirect instrument of knowledge: the antecedent simple perception produces subsequent perceptual judgement. The knowledge of linga acts as instrument for the knowledge of lingin; that of similarity is for upamiti and that of word for the knowledge of its meaning. The consideration of pramāṇa must also include unconscious objects like lamp, sense organs etc.

Buddhist View

Sautrāntikas and Vaibhāṣikas maintain that pramāṇa is that which gives true knowledge of objects or it is that which gives us the identity of content between the cognition and cognitum. The Yogācāra school accepts consciousness, the principle of self-manifestation as the source of all knowledge. Nāgārjuna refutes the existence of any pramāṇa whatsoever. Diṅnāga includes the characteristic of 'svasaṁvitti' meaning that the effect of a pramāṇa should involve self-cognition. (Svasaṁvittiḥ phalam cātra tadrūpārthaniścayaḥ viṣayākāra evāsya pramāṇam tena mīyate।)[16] The essence of pramāṇa, according to him, consists in the cognition of an object (Viṣayādhigama) and in self-cognition (Svasaṁvitti).

Jaina View

There is a considerable difference of opinion amongst the Jaina thinkers regarding the nature of pramāṇa. Siddhasena states that a pramāṇa is that which illumines itself and the object and which is not sublated. According to Akalaṅka, it is that which results in novel and uncontradicted knowledge. He also refers to the feature of pramāṇa, svaparabhāsaka — that which illumines itself and the object. Umāsvāti made no difference between jñāna and pramāṇa. He only mentions 'rightness' as the characteristic mark of pramāṇa. Maṇikyanandī maintains that jñāna is pramāṇa which has the determination of itself as well as of the object not known before. It enables us to get the desirable and give up the undesirable. Hemachandra states that the valid judgement about an object is pramāṇa. In other words, a means of knowledge is the authentic definitive cognition of an object.

Bhāṭṭa View

According to Kumārila, pramāṇa is a definite and assured cognition of objects which does not require confirmation by other cognitions. (Tasmāt dṛḍham yadutpannam nāpi saṁvādamṛcchati! Jñānāntareṇa vijñānam tatpramāṇam pramīyatam I I - Śloka-Vārtika - II - 80)[17].

Pārthasārathi explains the Bhāṭṭa standpoint saying that a pramāṇa should be free from defects in the source and subsequent contradiction of the revealed truth. It should not cover the knowledge of the already known objects. In short, according to Bhāṭṭas, a pramāṇa is a method of cognition of an object not already known which is not liable to be sublated by subsequent experience.

The Bhāṭṭas maintain that consciousness is not directly perceived or known. It is inferred through the fact of cognizedness of an object. Thus consciousness is an act according to them.

It is important to note that the Bhāṭṭa contention that pramāṇa is that which gives new knowledge (i.e. does not apprehend the already apprehended object) is not acceptable to many. Jayant maintains that whether a pramāṇa reveals a novel object or the already known object is immaterial. The collocation of conditions performs its function whatever the nature of object. The knowledge is always fresh even when the object revealed is old.

Moreover, Bhāṭṭa insistence upon anadhigatatva renders continuous knowledge (dhārāvāhika-jñāna) invalid. In this knowledge, the same object of knowledge persists. Hence, once the object is apprehended, its subsequent cognitions become invalid. Thus, anadhigatatva makes the definition of pramāna too narrow.

Another objection to novelty is that its acceptance will eliminate recognition as a form of valid knowledge. Recognition is the cognition of an object cognised before.

According to Jayanta, it is not necessary to insert the condition of a novelty in order to eliminate memory from the means of valid knowledge. The purpose will be served even if we insert the word 'arthajanyatva' (produced by the object or produced on the basis of object).

Sāṁkhya View

According to the Sāṁkhya view, pramāṇa is a modification of Buddhi. Kapila maintains that pramāṇa is what is conducive to the determinate knowledge of an object not known before. Vācaspati holds that pramāṇa is a modification of citta having a content free from all that is doubtful and erroneous. Iśvarakṛṣṇa simply maintains that pramāṇa is that which brings about the cognition of objects.

Viśiṣṭādvaita View of Pramāṇa

Even in Viśiṣṭādvaita, the word pramāṇa is used in two senses. Its means valid knowledge and also instruments of valid knowledge; this distinction corresponds to Karaṇaprāmāṇya and āśrayaprāmāṇya. In the sense of instrument, pramāṇa is that which leads to valid knowledge. In the case of perception for example, those which would lead to valid knowledge would be defectless eyes, mind-contact as attention, proper proximity of the object etc. and these would jointly constitute pramāṇa. But in the case of testimony, it is the faultlessness of the speaker that constitutes validity. The scriptures are valid because they are uttered by God, who has the right knowledge of things. The ultimate determination of pramāṇa is through pramā, or right knowledge.

Vātsya Śrīnivāsa defines pramāṇa (in the sense of means of knowledge as the most efficient instrument amongst a collocation of causes forming the immediate, invariable and unconditional antecedents of any right knowledge. Thus, in the case of perception, for example, the visual organ is a pramāṇa which leads to right visual knowledge through its intermediary vyāpāra — the sense contact of the eye with its object. It is obvious that such a view differs from Nyāya view according to which the collocation of all causal factors (and not any one particular most efficient factor therefrom) is the pramāṇa.

Mādhva View

Madhvā has done a distinct service to Indian Epistemology in distinguishing two senses of the word pramāṇa and coining two separate terms 'kevala' and 'anu' pramāṇa to denote these two senses. He defines pramāṇa in both the above senses as yathārtham — not going beyond the knowable object, i.e. revealing the nature of an object as it really is: (Yathāvasthitajñeyaviṣayīkāri).

Pramāṇa in its first sense (of valid knowledge) refers to the capacity of true knowledge to reveal the nature of an object as it really is. As applied to pramāṇa in its second sense (of means of valid knowledge), it means the means by which such a correct knowledge is obtained. But there is no difference in the directness of their relation to their objects. Both Kevala pramāṇa and anu- pramāṇa function with same immediacy. But the instruments produce jñeyatā in jñana while jñāna merely acts as a manifesting condition thereof. Hence the two classifications are based upon their respective mode of relation to knowability.

Jayatīrtha defines pramāṇa as the knowledge of a thing as it actually is, with reference to a particular space-time setting; it is knowledge which answers to the nature of the thing. But here correspondence only means Yāvadāveditasya sattvam or the existence of such aspects as are actually perceived by each person according to the extent of his capacity or understanding and other conditions governing the rapprochement to the object.

(C) Individual Pramāṇas

Pramāṇas

The analysis of the concept of pramāṇa takes us to the next problem: The nature and peculiarities of individual pramāṇas. We have to deal with them separately in order to decide whether they are genuine and independent or not.

Perception

Almost all systems of Indian philosophy agree that perception is a process which is initiated by the contact of an object with the sense-organ and culminates in the arousal of the awareness of the object of the part of the self. This contact is the peculiar cause of perceptual knowledge and as such constitutes the differentiam of perception as a means of cognition. The distinction between indeterminate and determinate perception is well-known in the field of Indian epistemology. Indeterminate perception refers to the awareness of an object which is non-relational and non-judgemental. Determinate perception is the awareness of an object with its genus, name, quality etc. Almost all orthodox schools accepts this distinction between two independent forms of perception. It is obvious that the problem of validity and invalidity can arise only in the case of determinate perception which alone is relational and judgemental in nature.

Perception is also distinguished into external and internal depending upon two kinds of sensible objects and two kinds of sense-organs. In the internal perception, mind or antaḥkarṇa is accepted as a sense-organ responsible for the awareness of pleasure, pain, aversion, cognition etc. Mādhvas accept memory as a kind of internal perception or mānasapratyakṣa. Even Jainas accept memory as a variety of empirical perception.

Generally six kinds of normal or ordinary perception are admitted; but Jainas, Naiyāyikas and some members of Sāṁkhya school accept what is called extraordinary perception or alaukika pratyakṣa. According to Naiyāyikas, sāmānya-lakṣaṇa, jñāna-lakṣaṇa and yogaja are three varieties of extraordinary perception. Both sāmānya-lakṣaṇa and jñāna-lakṣaṇa presuppose earlier experience of the objects and memory of that experience.

In fact, perception in general also involves the use of memory. Perception, at its first instance is vague and indefinite. But when it is interpreted and becomes definite, its definiteness is largely due to memory. The analysis of perceptual data, classification, identification are made possible by memory.

A variety of perception, viz. recognition (pratyabhijñā) depends upon memory to even a greater extent. It has two important elements: the present perception of an object and its remembrance as the same as perceived in the past. Mere perception cannot contribute both these elements.

Inference

Inference is a source of cognition and also a way of reasoning. As a source of cognition, it produces inferential knowledge, i.e. anumiti. It creates the awareness of an object through the consideration of a mark which is invariably connected with the object of knowledge. This invariable connection or concomitance is the backbone of inference. Once it is established, the sensuous presentation of mark (liṅga) leads to the awareness of the object of knowledge (liṅgī). This invariable concomitance or universal generalisation is based upon simple enumeration and also the extraordinary perception of universal aspect of things.

Inferences are classified into svāthānumāna (inference for oneself) and parārthānumāna (inference for the sake of others). The former is a psychogenetic account of inferential knowledge and it involves the knowledge and memorisation of the relation of invariable concomitance between a liṅga and liṅgī, perception of liṅga and consequent apprehension of liṅgī. The parārthānumāna is the formal demonstration of truths.

Inferences are also classified into pūrvavat, śeṣavat and sāmānyatodṛṣṭa depending upon the nature of vyāpti — whether it is causal or non-causal in nature.

Uddyotakāra introduces one more classification of inferences into anvayī, vyatirekī and anvayavyatirekī depending upon the nature of vyāpti, whether it refers to uniformity in presence or absence or both.

Whatever the variety of inference, it depends upon the revival of the impressions of the previous knowledge of vyāpti. Memory thus plays a key-role in it. The inferential knowledge is not derived from memory alone, but it is impossible to get it in the absence of the memory of vyāpti.

Testimony — Śabda

Literal meaning of Śabda is 'word', but as an independent source of cognition, Śabda means statements of authority which is reliable. The Buddhists and the Vaiśeṣikas reject testimony as an independent source of knowledge arguing that it is an instance of inference from the trustworthiness of the authority and from the invariable concomitance between words and their meaning.

According to D.M. Datta, the process of verbal cognition or Testimony involves the following stages:

(1) The sensation of sound (2) The interpretation of sound (3) Recognition of the meaning signified by each word (when sounds are words or symbols of thought) (4) A constructive

apprehension of the different independent meanings presented by different words (5) Belief in the truth of the meaning of the sentence uttered.

The third and the fourth stage seem to be specially dependent upon memory. Whether the meaning of a word is grasped as a whole or through the combination of the meaning of its individual members, the part played by memory is undeniable. The primary meaning is grasped only through memory. The knowledge of secondary and tertiary meaning requires other knowledges in addition to memory, like the motive of the speaker etc.

Even as regards the meaning of a sentence, the Prābhākaras insist that it is known through, memory, since the meaning is presented by words themselves, which are remembered to possess certain meanings. Even Bhāṭṭas who insist that the knowledge of the meaning of a sentence is construed out of the meanings presented by the words and hence is a new kind of knowledge admit that it is usually built on the material supplied by memory.

Testimony is classified into Laukika (statements of reliable persons) and Alaukika (scriptural statements). Even Jainism accepts laukika (secular) and lokottara (non-secular) testimony but points that the validity of secular testimony cannot be guaranteed. Its truth of falsity would depend upon the excellence (guṇa) or imperfection (doṣa) of the speaker.

Comparison — Upamāna

According to the Nyāya school, upamiti, i.e. knowledge from comparison is the knowledge of the denotative relation between a word or a name standing for an unfamiliar object and the unfamiliar object itself. The ground for this knowledge is the resemblance between the unfamiliar object and the already familiar one. Thus an individual is already familiar with the ordinary cow. He is told by an elderly person that a wild cow (gavaya) resembles an ordinary cow. Walking through the forest, he sees a strange animal, perceives it to be similar to a cow, remembers the words of the elderly person and acquires the knowledge that gavaya is the name of the strange animal.

It is thus a complicated process which involves Testimony, Perception and Memory.

Mīmāṁsā and Vedānta schools suggest a different view of upamāna. According to them upamiti is the knowledge of resemblance of an unperceived object to the perceived one. The moment we know that the remembered cow is similar to the perceived gavaya, the process of upamāna is complete. Even this account of upamāna involves perception and memory as essential factors. In fact memory plays such an important role in this account of upamāna that the Vaiśeṣika school refuses to treat this as an independent source of cognition and instead treats it as an instance of recollection. It insists that since domestic cow is remembered, its similarity to any other object is also remembered. An interesting point to be noted in this context is that the resultant knowledge which is accepted as valid by all, has been equally satisfactorily traced to perception, memory and comparison.

In other words, almost everyone accepts the knowledge through comparison as valid but there is a difference of opinion whether this knowledge is through comparison or perception or memory. This implies that memory-knowledge has as much validity as belonging to perceptual knowledge and knowledge through comparison.

Presumption — Arthāpatti

This source of knowledge is accepted only by Mīmāṃsā and Vedānta schools of philosophy. Mīmāṃsakas define it as the assumption of an unperceived fact apart from which the conflict between two actually perceived facts cannot be resolved. Prabhākara insists that presumption involves an element of doubt about the truth of two well-known facts on account of their mutual conflict. The specific function of presumption is to remove the doubt. According to Kumārila, presumption involves conflict between two well known facts and is also required to resolve it. According to the Vedānta school, presumption means framing of an explanatory hypothesis on the basis of the knowledge of the fact to be explained.

It is a process through which we obtain the knowledge of a fact that explains what is otherwise inexplicable. The instances of arthāpatti are of two kinds: dṛṣṭārthāpatti and śrutārthāpatti. The first means supposition of a fact in order to explain visually perceived (seen) facts. The second means supposition of a fact in order to explain a fact known through testimony.

It is obvious that whatever the variety of arthāpatti, a supposition can be made only on the basis of memory. A missing connection between two conflicting facts is not given by perception nor by inference but by memory. That of which we have not had earlier experience and consequent impression cannot occur to us in the form of a supposition.

Non-Apprehension : Anupalabdhi

Bhāṭṭas and Vedāntins accept non-apprehension as a source of knowledge. This is done to account for the knowledge of non-existence of something which itself is treated as a separate category. The argument is that while as existence can be known through perception, the knowledge of non-existence or absence is derived through another source and that is anupalabdhi. The non-existence of an object is not identical with its locus but is something additional to it. Even Naiyāyikas accept the separate category of non-existence, but believe that it can be known through perception. According to Bhāṭṭas and Advaitins, non-cognition is a pramāṇa which gives knowledge of non existence.

The question is: Does every non-cognition give knowledge of non-existence? The answer is in the negative. Only an appropriate non-cognition gives knowledge of non-existence. But how to decide the appropriateness? The non-cognition is appropriate when we can ascertain that the object not known would have been known, had it been present there, under those very circumstances. Thus for example, the awareness that had the jar been present, it would have been known through any one of the means of valid knowledge, under those very conditions, renders the non-cognition appropriate. But this awareness itself is derived from the memory of earlier experiences of jar and hence the role played by memory in anupalabdhi is undeniably important.

Other Minor Sources of Cognition

Aitihya or Tradition means body of traditional beliefs originating from unknown sources and handed down from generation to generation. Saṁbhava is a process of knowing something indirectly and mediately on account of its being included in something already known. Ceṣṭā or gesture is accepted by the Tāntrikas as a source of cognition. Bodily gestures and facial expressions convey meaning Pariśeṣa or elimination is a process of knowing something by means of the elimination from a group of objects of those which are distinct from it.

With this, the discussion of pramāṇas comes to an end. This is done primarily with a view to ascertain the nature and peculiarities of each individual pramāṇa, the general criteria to be satisfied by pramāṇas as such and the role played by memory in the basic and generally accepted pramāṇas.

The question now is : Can memory satisfy these criteria of prāmāṇya? Or, is it merely an element in each cognitive process like perception, inference etc.? A satisfactory answer to this question requires complete analysis of the nature of memory as done by philosophers as well as psychologists both in the West as well as in India.

References

1. 'Perception' by B.K. Matilal, p. 100-112.
2. Sarvaryavaharahetuḥ I Tarkasaṁgraha by Annam Bhaṭṭa-Sutra 34.
3. Nyāyamañjari, p. 12.
4. Quoted by Jitendranath Mohanty — Gaṅgeśa's Theory of Truth, p. 42.
5. Tarka-saṁgraha Sutra, 35, p. 23.
6. Quoted by Jitendranath Mohanty — Gaṅgeśa's Theory of Truth, p. 9.
7. Ibid.
8. Ibid. p. 18.
9. Philosophy of Madhvācārya — B.N.Sharma, p. 128-129, Rev. Edn.

10. Nyāya-pariśuddhi, p. 90 as quoted by S.M. Srinivasachari — Fundamentals of Visistadvaita Vedanta, p. 73.
11. "Śrī Rāmānuja's Theory of Knowledge — A Study" by Dr. K.C. Varadachari, p. 182.
12. Quoted by B.N.K. Sharma — Philosophy of Madhvācārya, p. 127, Rev. Edn.
13. Indian Theory of Knowledge — C.D. Bijalwan, p. 40.
14. Nyāyamañjari-I-12 by Jayant Bhaṭṭa.
15. Nyāyamañjari-I-14.
16. Pramāṇa-Samuccaya-I-10.
17. Indian Theory of Knowledge by C.D. Bijalwan, p. 45.

Chapter IV

The Nature of Memory-Part I

Views of Western Thinkers

Among various sources of knowledge of facts, memory is one. Like other sources, even the word memory may refer to the knowledge itself as a product (phala) or the instrument which results in the knowledge (karaṇa). Thus we may indiscriminately say, "My memory is correct" or "It is a result of memory".

It is a problem worth careful consideration and analysis if memory can be accepted as a source of valid knowledge. But even before we analyse it, it is worth our while to analyse the concept of memory, as understood by philosophers as well as psychologists.

The word "remember' appears in many different grammatical constructions, and takes a wide variety of grammatical objects. One can remember an event, an action, a person, a place, a feeling, a procedure, a line of verse, a melody or a person's name. One can remember doing something, seeking something or thinking something. And one can remember where something is, when a certain event happened, who did a certain thing etc. One may also remember facts about future, facts about the present, scientific laws and generalisations and truths of logic and mathematics.

Thus the word admits of a variety of uses. But philosophers have generally concerned themselves with memory of facts about remembered events. This kind of memory is distinguished from habit-memory or memory of how to do something. Habit-memory is simply the retention of a motor mechanism and differs from memory par excellence or what Russell calls 'true memory' which alone is cognitive in nature.

The classical theories of memory have treated it as a mental occurrence taking place in the present and it is a source of knowledge concerning the past. (Some recent analysts have challenged this contention and have stressed upon memory dispositions or memory powers).

In Western philosophy, various theories analysing the nature of memory have been suggested. The most dominant has been the representative theory and there is also the theory given by the naive realists.

According to the representative theory, someone's remembering a past event consists at least partly in his apprehending something that is not past, that is, something occurring at the time at which the person has memory. It is something private to the individual; it is a content of his mind which is variously called an 'image' a 'presentation' and 'idea' and the 'immediate' or 'present' object in memory. This 'image' is not the object of memory; but it is the present object through which past event is remembered. It serves as a sign or a picture of the remembered object, and is accepted as evidence for the rememberer to know that such an event has occurred.

Sometimes it is also believed that memory presentations are impressions stored in the memory. Thus Locke said that memory is, "as it were the store-house of our ideas' in which the ideas are 'as it were laid out of sight'. In the second edition (of the Essay concerning human understanding) however he added that, "this laying up of our ideas in the repository of the memory signifies no more but this— that the mind has a power in many cases to revive perceptions which it has once had, with this additional perception annexed to them, that it has had them before.'[1] Thus even here Locke suggests that the same thing is first presented in sense-impression and later revived in memory. Even Hume holds that when any impression has been present with the mind, it again makes its appearance there as an idea". Both Locke and Hume are clear that the memory-image of a past perception is not that perception itself, it is a numerically different perception which can represent the past perception.

As a representative theorist, Hume thinks it necessary to make distinction between memory and imagination both of which make use of images. He states that ideas of memory are "much more lively and strong than those of the imagination have a 'superior force and vivacity'. In other words, memory involves belief in the previous occurrence of impressions and also the belief that they had the same order and form as that of the ideas. The second difference between two is that in imagination ideas need not occur in the same order as that of the original impressions; but the order of the ideas in memory cannot vary from that of the original impressions.

Memory must have then, belief as one of its features. It is not something imagined or supposed. It is also marked by the awareness that it is something in the past or something previously experienced by the remember. Both Bertrand Russell and William James (whose analysis of memory will be examined in detail later) have made this feeling of pastness an essential constituent of memory. Russell also speaks of feeling of familiarity. Remembering is a present occurrence in some way resembling what is remembered. This consists partly in the occurrence of images and also our belief that they are more or less correct copies of past occurrences.

Naive Realism

The alternative to representative theory of memory is assumed to be naive realism. According to this theory what one is directly aware of in memory is the remembered event itself and not a mere representation of it. Samuel Alexander whose views on memory we are going to examine in detail later, holds that when one remembers something, the object of memory is 'before the mind, bearing on its face the mark of pastness'[2] and H.H. Price once held that "some memory is knowledge in the strict sense, i.e. is direct or immediate apprehension of past events or situations"[3].

The explanation given by naive realism has an advantage over the representative account of memory. It does not have to explain how we are justified in inferring the past event from the present memory datum, because there is no such inference of the past event itself.

Difficulties Associated with Representationism

Both representative theory and naive realists' theory of memory have their share of difficulties. According to Reid, to hold a kind of relationship between impressions and ideas (as the representative theory of Hume does) can only mean that we remember that our impressions are frequently followed by ideas which resemble them. But this would involve having memory-knowledge of the past that is not inferred from the present ideas. For inferring the past events from the present ones, we need to know certain empirical generalisations. And such generalisations can be discovered only if we have immediate and non-inferential knowledge of the past. Associating an idea with a past impression is not to remember the past impression.

In fact, representative theory is criticised as making the knowledge of the past impossible. Reid holds that if ideas are the only immediate objects of thought then we will require arguments to prove that the ideas of memory are pictures of things that really did happen. It wil be impossible to get arguments that will have real weight. In short, there is no possible explanation of how to take a certain present experience as indicating the existence of such and such past events.

Difficulties associated with Naive Realism

The main difficulty connected with naive realism is determining the exact sense of direct awareness' of the past. We cannot be aware of the past in the sense in which we are directly aware of our pains or mental images; because then we just cannot be wrong regarding the awareness of the past'. If again, this direct awareness means remembering is a mode of awareness where no other memory is involved, then this is a truism no one wants to reject. Or perhaps, direct awareness of the past means that memory knowledge of the past is immediate in the sense of not being inferred from or grounded on private memory data. It is argued that such an interpretation of 'direct awareness' does not really explain memory-knowledge. It simply asserts that we have memory-knowledge which is immediate but does not state how we have it.

A more detailed analysis of these two important views on memory and difficulties associated with each needs to be done. But prior to that we will do well to ascertain in detail the views on memory of some eminent Western thinkers—philosophers, philosopher-psychologists and psychologists. This is not to suggest that we have such a clear-cut division among thinkers; it rather points out that certain ways of thinking and analysing problems are more prominently displayed than other ways by these thinkers. Our subsequent sections contain such views.

Views of Philosophers

Bertrand Russell

Russell introduces the problem of 'knowledge' before going into the details of memory. He points out that the concept of knowledge is often treated as though its meaning were obvious and unitary. But actually many philosophical difficulties and controversies arise from insufficient realisation of the differences between different kinds of knowledge. We are also vague and uncertain about what we believe ourselves to know. He insists that in the analysis of any mental concepts, our evolutionary continuity with the lower animals ought not to be forgotton; we should not define knowledge in such a manner as to assume an impassable gulf between ourselves and our ancestors who did not have the advantage of language.

He distinguishes between knowledge of facts and knowledge of the general connections between facts. This distinction is closely connected with another distinction: Knowledge which is mirroring and knowledge which consists in capacity to handle.

Our knowledge of facts, in so far as it is not inferential, has two sources, sensation and memory. Of these, sensation is more fundamental because only that can be remembered what is already perceived.

Memory is described as the purest kind of mirror-knowledge or the knowledge of facts. Our state of mind in memory is very similar to the state of mind in perception. In fact even according to psychologists, there are no clear criteria to distinguish memory from perception. In his own words: "When I remember a piece of music or a friend's face, my state of mind resembles, though with a difference, what it was when I heard the music or saw the face. . .a considerable degree of credibility attaches to a memory on its own account, particularly if it is vivid and recent".[4]

Thus memory introduces us to knowledge in one of its forms. The analysis of memory-knowledge becomes necessary both as an introduction to the problem of knowledge and because memory in some form is presupposed in almost all other knowledge.

Memory judgements can be looked upon as self-evident or intuitive judgements. This class includes those judgements for which no justifying reason can be given, and it includes such principles as that of induction or logical principles used in constructing demonstration.

The other kind of self-evident truths are those immediately derived from sensation. These truths of perception may be simple or complex (They cannot be sense-data which just are and truths are obtained from them).

Memory poses a problem which one does not face in sensation. Memory of an object is apt to be accompanied by an image of the object, and yet the image itself does not constitute memory. Image is perceived in the present but what is remembered is known to be in the past. Moreover, we can also know whether our image is accurate or not by comparing it with the object remembered. Thus the essence of memory is not constituted by the image. There must be, then intuitive judgements of memory and it is upon them that ultimately all our knowledge of past depends. But for the fact of memory in this sense we should not know that there ever was a past; in fact we would not even understand the word 'past'.

Apart from its being accompanied by an image, there is another difficulty raised by memory which is discussed in detail by Russell. ". . .for it is notoriously fallacious, and thus throws doubt on the trustworthiness of intuitive judgements in general. This difficulty is no light one."[5]

At the same time Russell points out that memory is trustworthy in proportion to the vividness of experience and to its nearness in time. The memory of most recent and the most vivid events must be trustworthy because of its obvious self-evidence.

Going backward in time to remembered events or to less vivid experiences, memory becomes less self-evident and less trustworthy. There is a continual gradation in the degree of self-evidence of what we remember and the corresponding gradation of the trustworthiness of our memory.

"Thus the first answer to the difficulty of fallacious memory is to say that memory has degrees of self-evidence, and that these correspond to the degrees of its trustworthiness, reaching a limit of perfect self-evidence and perfect trustworthiness in our memory of events which are recent and vivid".[6]

It is possible to have cases of very firm belief in a memory which is wholly false. It is probable that in these cases what is remembered is something other than what is falsely believed in, though something generally associated with it. In other words, the cases of fallacious memory can be shown to be not cases of memory in the strict sense at all.

The memory-images, then can account for the knowledge of the past, provided the memory itself has self-evidence and consequent trustworthiness. These, in turn, are determined by vividness and nearness in time of the original experience.

It must be borne in mind that everything constituting memory-belief is happening in the present. Secondly, these images without beliefs cannot constitute memory. The images are believed as more or less accurate copies of original. One characteristic which inspires this belief or confidence is the feeling of familiarity. Some images feel very familiar, others feel very strange. This feeling is capable of degrees. We have more belief in the accuracy of those parts of the memory-image with which we are more familiar. The other characteristic which memory-images must have in order to account for our knowledge of the past is their referring to more or less remote portions of the past. It is called feeling of pastness. Familiarity leads us to trust our memories; pastness leads us to assign places to them in time-order.

Thus in true memory, the process of remembering consists of calling up images of our original experience; which will come to us with a feeling of belief such as distinguishes memory-images from mere imagination-images. This feeling of belief may be expressed in the words, "this happened". This belief-feeling can be distinguished from other belief-feeling associated with expectation and bare assent. The content believed may or may not be expressed in words.

Russell, thus accepts memory as a source of valid knowledge of the past. This, he calls true memory. It is accompanied by images which by themselves do not constitute its essence. They have a kind of an immediacy, self-evidence and therefore trustworthiness. The image must be accompanied by a feeling of belief expressible as "this occurred". This belief or confidence is inspired by a feeling of familiarity and that of pastness. The points really important for our purpose may be repeated in Russell's own words: ". . .our. . .indubitable data is that there is knowledge of the past. Whatever the arguments of the sceptic, we cannot practically doubt that we know the past and that memory forms an indispensable part of our knowledge of the past. Second datum is that we certainly have more capacity for knowing the past than for knowing the future. Our knowledge of the future, whatever we have, is a matter of elaborate calculation and inference, while as some of our knowledge of the past is without effort having some immediacy which our present sense-experience has. Memory seems to be a way of knowing about the past which has no analogue in our knowledge of the future".[7]

Samuel Alexander

Alexander admits the immediate perception of the pastness of an object in memory. In remembering certain things or events, we are aware that we have experienced them before. While as William James maintains that the object of memory is only an object imagined in the past to which the emotion of belief adheres, Alexander makes only a slight change and says that the object of memory is an object imagined or thought of in 'my' past; the change is necessary because I may believe in the past events without really being able to remember them. "The object, then, is before my mind, bearing on its face the mark of pastness, of being earlier than those objects which I call present. In the mind there corresponds to it the act of imagining or conveiving it, and there is in addition the act of remembering it, the consciousness that I have had it before".[8]

The pastness of the object is a datum of experience, directly apprehended. The object is compresent in us as past. The act of remembering is a process whereby this object becomes attached to ourselves (or appropriated by ourselves) by our present consciousness of ourselves.

In this present consciousness of ourselves, we may distinguish a subjective and a bodily element unified in the person. The past object is earlier than our present act of mind in remembering, or our equivalent bodily state. When the past object is thus appropriated by ourselves, we are aware of it as belonging to us, as ours, as occurring in our past. This is the consciousness that the object is remembered. Just as we are aware of a perceived object when we have before us a sensory experience, we have memory when we have before us an experience of the past and appropriate it to our personality. The object, then belonghs to such a past in which we contemplate ourselves having been existent also and related to the object.

Like a single perception, a single memory is incomplete. The particular percept is full of movement towards other aspects of the thing perceived, and the memory, similarly throws out feelers to other memories. Our memory of the whole thing is built by these memories through their internal coherence and continuity.

But we need not have this whole thing before us in memory. We may only have before us its appearance altered by the lapse of time and seen through the haze of time. We may also add to this the subjective prejudices of the experient. But it remains what it declares itself to be, nothing but the revelation of thing through the mist of intervening time.

A.J. Ayer

Ayer's views on memory are worth noting because he brings out a novel consideration in his analysis of memory. He points out that our reliance on memory is an important factor in the forming of our idea of the causal direction of events. Memory exemplifies our ability to take note of what has has happened; therefore while we think we know something about the future we rightly think that we know a great deal more about the past.

We think that we can strive to bring things about or that we can affect the future course of events but not the past events, because the past events are already known to exist. The future events are yet to exist, therefore human action is thought of as essentially forward-moving. But this direction is determined by our memory.

Memory to which Ayer refers here is the factual memory or memory of events. To begin with, he makes distinction between factual memory and habit memory. Habitual memory consists in one's having the power to reproduce a certain performance and it does not require one to recall any past occurrence. The class of habit-memory is pretty extensive. It includes not only those instances of knowing how to do things, but also a great many instances in which knowledge displayed is classified as knowledge of facts. It may involve the use of images, but it may as well dispense with images. Even when the images occur, they do so as aids to memory and do not themselves constitute memory. To remember is simply to be able to state facts. However, this kind of memory does not give knowledge of the past, and if it does, then it is only incidentally.

But habitual memory ultimately rests upon the fact that someone remembers that something was so. This remembering consists in recollecting a past event. "And surely memory in this sense is a source of knowledge. The evidence that the past event occurred is to be found in the character of one's present-memory experience."[9]

Ayer, further analyses the nature of this kind of memory or rather, memory-experience. Generally, factual memory is believed to consist of a distinctive sort of image. Others, like Russell insist that this image must be accompanied by a feeling of familiarity in order to become a memory image.

But Ayer points out that image may be a necessary feature of the memory of events seen. But in the case of other senses, there are no images. Even in the case of things seen, there may not always be some present image in the mind. In fact, the better one's memory functions, the more readily one states the past facts without any intervening images.

Images appear to play only an auxiliary role. They may have very little resemblance to the past event; they may even be very 'bad' images; in memory-experience we never compare images with the original; we as it were see the original through the images. A present image can refer to the past event because it is so interpreted. We so interpret it that it prompts us to form an accurate belief about our past experience.

Ayer then goes on to establish that there is no sharp distinction between habit-memory and factual memory, since in former the images may be at times used and in latter they may be at times dispensed with. In both we show the ability to give appropriate performance whether of displaying the skill or of stating the fact. The factual memory is marked by the true belief that the experience occurred, and occurred in one's own past.

In this context, Ayer examines the theory of naive realists and points out that 'the direct acquaintance with the past' does not really explain the fact of memory. Nor does he accept Prof. C.D. Broad's argument that an event which is past continues to exist for all time. According to Ayer, our conception of past is determined by our conception of present and that of temporal precedence. He insists that our statements about past need not be interpreted as the statements about present and future for the sake of their verification. The statements about the past can be justified on the basis of inductive argument. We believe that the future processes continue to grow out of past. We account for the later event by correlating it with the earlier event. This is done on the basis of some general hypothesis which itself may make an appeal to memory. For instance, we assume that people are commonly in a position to know about the events which they claim to remember. Their statements can be cross-checked. Then there are canons of historical evidence. One authority can be checked against another; psychological and economic laws can be brought into play, thus in a considerable number of cases the evidence attains a strength which makes it proper to say that some statement about an earlier event is known to be true. This is roughly the nature of inductive argument which justifies our statements about past based upon memory.

From Ayer's analysis of memory, it is obvious that though he is aware of the limitations of memory, yet from time to time, he accepts it as a source of knowledge, its knowledge being verifiable through inductive argument and its determining influence in the formation of our idea of the causal direction of events.

Views of Philosopher-Psychologists

In this section we intend to state the views of some philosopher-psychologists like William James and G.F. Stout. They have analysed the mechanism of memory and have also philosophically analysed memory as a source of knowledge, the explanation of its pastness, validity of its knowledge.

William James

According to William James the memory of some of our thoughts survives the instant of their passage. Of others, it is confined to a few moments, hours or days. Some thoughts leave impressions which are indestructible and they help the recall of thoughts as long as life endures.

"Memory proper is the knowledge of a former state of mind after it has already once dropped from consciousness, or rather it is the knowledge of an event or fact of which meantime we have not been thinking, with the additional consciousness that we have thought or experienced it before".[10]

The first element such a knowledge would seem to involve is a mental image. It is this mental image which distinguishes secondary memory (or memory proper) from primary memory. Primary memory contains after-image or a kind of continuous sensation. It vanishes in a few seconds. It makes us aware of the just past. But this primary memory is not recollection proper, as it does not belong to the genuine past. In secondary memory (or memory proper) the object is absent from consciousness altogether and is then revived-with the help of memory-image. This requires that the original impression should have been prolonged enough to give rise to a recurrent image.

But mere revival of an image is obviously not memory. Image is but a duplicate, a second event and no memory is involved in the mere fact of recurrence.

A further condition is therefore, required before the present image can be held to stand for a past original.

That condition is that the fact imaged be expressly referred to the past, thought as in the past but a past event can be thought of only with a lot of contiguous associates—like names or other symbols or some concrete events.

But even this would not be memory, according to James. It needs something more than mere dating of a fact in the past. "It must be dated in my past. In other words, I must think that I directly experienced its occurrence. It must have the 'warmth' and 'intimary' of all the experiences appropriated by the thinker as his own."[11]

These are then the important elements of which every memory is made up. It involves a general feeling of the past direction in time, a particular date conveived as lying along that direction; the date being definable by its name or its association with certain events, an event imagined as located therein and owned as part of my experience.

Thus memory is not any simple-shaped image. It is a feeling of belief in a complex object, a representation of the fact plus its associates. This particular relation of belief- feeling to ourselves is what gives uniqueness to memory of the fact plus its associates.

According to James, the complete exercise of memory presupposes two things—

(i) Retention of the remembered fact.

(ii) Its reminiscence or recollection.

The cause of both of retention and recollection is the law of habit in the nervous system, working as it does in the association of ideas. When we are making search in our memory for a forgotten idea, we turn over the ideas with which or alongside of which, it may possibly be; and if it lies near them, it soon comes to view.

Even retention (liability to recall) can be explained by the same machinery—the law of association or the law of habit. We have the tendency to think the experience again with its past surroundings. This is made possible by the organised neutral paths by which the cue calls up the experience on the proper occasion. The excellence of memory depends upon the number and the persistence of paths. More the paths from to the fact, prompter and surer is the memory. In other words, more the facts the given fact is connected with, better possession of it our memory retains.

Thus, according to James, memory has different durations in different instances; memory proper is bringing before consciousness what has totally lapsed behind; it contains a general feeling of past direction of time; an event dated in the past and marked by various associates; its belonging to past and specially my past and accompanied by a general feeling of belief. It presupposes retention and recollection both of which can be explained by laws of association.

G.F. Stout

According to G.F. Stout, in remembering past events, we have a knowledge which is immediate in the sense that it is not inferential or representative in any ordinary meaning of these terms. He further maintains that in thus remembering, we do not actually experience what we remember in the process of remembering it. What is actually or immediately experienced belongs to our present and is not apprehended as past or future. While we are remembering, the remembering is an actual experience. But the past which is remembered as such is not actually experienced in remembering it.

But still it must be admitted that memory-knowledge of the past is logically rooted and grounded in actual present experience. Apart from this it has no independent footing. The appeal to memory is an appeal to what we are now actually experiencing "...in the act of remembering, what we presently and actually experience is essentially imcomplete and cannot be apprehended at all except as continued from its own past. Indeed remembrance is as indispensable to knowledge of the present as such as it is to knowledge of the past as such".[12]

Right at the outset Stout specifies the meaning of the otherwise ambiguous word 'memory'. He confines it to reminiscence which is a primary way of knowing past events as such. The ordinary usage of 'memory' also covers retentiveness in general which is an indispensable condition of the unity and continuity of individual experience. Even the reminiscence is not just of past occurrences but of past occurrences in the individual's own mental history.

Again, remembering is not actuallly living through the bygone experience as it actually occurred. It is impossible to actually or immediately experience what we remember as past, and this holds universally for all reminiscences properly so called. In all reminiscence there is a difference between the past and the present and this difference acts as a bar to their union in the same moment of actual experience.

The original content and retained content are different but only as successive stages in the history of the same thing. In immediately experiencing a memory-image we are aware of it as continued from a past impression or past impressions. "Both memory-image and past impressions are occurrents in the history of what relatively to them is a 'continuant'. How far they resemble each other is a secondary though an important question".[13]

But though in remembering the past, we do not actually or immediately experience it, still we can immediately know it. Knowing immediately does not mean that in this knowledge there is nothing intervening between the knowing mind and what is known. Stout refuses to accept any representative account of knowledge, including memory-knowledge. In his own words, "There is no knowing what is represented without knowing its relation to what represents it, and this pre-supposes a knowledge of both which must ultimately be immediate and cannot itself be representative".[14] Knowing immediately also does not mean to actually experience at the time we take cognisance of the fact, as for example, when we know toothache.

To say that we have immediate memory-knowledge is to say that we have non-inferential memory-knowledge. Inferential knowledge is always mediate knowledge.

According to Stout, there are judgements the evidence for which is contained within themselves (this is not the case with the judgements which are inferred) in such a way that it cannot be extracted and asserted by itself in a distinct proposition. Such judgements may be universal or particular matters of fact. Memory judgements are of the latter kind where internal ground for the judgement is some particular matter of fact; in the case of memory judgement, internal ground is a character of actual present experience. But this character or internal ground is not capable of being known by itself in such a way as to be asserted in a proposition distinct from the memory judgement.

The last and an equally important question which Stout asks and answers is: How far are memory judgements trustworthy? In one sense, according to him, they are all infallible. All of them yield a presumption that the past is such as we remember it to have been. But this presumption has differing grades of strength in differing memory judgements; the reason is that the character of the actual experience on which memory judgements are based is determined by retentiveness and the operation of retentiveness itself is determined by a variety of conditions. Stout argues that it would be a tenable position to say that all memory judgements are probable; but he himself does not hold that all memory judgements are only probable. According to him it is an arbitrary assumption that memory of the past may approach speculative certainty but can never reach it. There is no general evidence to refute or to support such a thesis. Secondly, there is an overwhelming evidence to show that at least some of our memory judgements are absolutely certain.

Thomas Reid

Reid regards memory as a kind of faculty belonging to human beings which is unfolded soon after the faculty of perception. It is a faculty by which we have an immediate knowledge of things past. The senses give us information of things only as they exist in the present moment. If this information is not preserved by memory, it would vanish instantly and we would be as ignorant as if it had never been.

Reid mentions some more things which are obvious and certain with regard to memory. Every remembrance has its object. The object of remembrance must be distinguished from the act of remembrance which takes place in the present. The object of memory must always be past; what now is, cannot be an object of memory. Memory is always accompanied with the belief of that which we remember. A man can give no other reason of his belief but that he remembers the thing distinctly. In his own words, "This belief, which we have from distinct memory, we account real knowledge, no less certain than if it was grounded on demonstration; no man in his wits calls it in question or will hear any argument against it. . .all the knowledge of mankind of past events is built on this foundation".[15]

Our acquisition of the notion of duration is due to memory. When we remember a thing, we also believe in some interval of duration that has passed between the time it happened and the present mement when it is remembered.

The remembrance of a past event is necessarily accompanied with the conviction of our own existence at the time the thing happened. It is impossible to remember a past thing without a strong conviction that I, the same identical person who now remembers that event, did then exist. The proper evidence for a permanent self which has a claim to all the thoughts, actions and feelings which we call ours is our remembrance. Our memory not only testifies that these things were done but also that they were done by us who now remember them. If these things were done by us who now remember them, we must have existed at that time and must have continued to exist from that time to the present. Thus our knowledge of personal identity is also due to memory. Memory does not merely give knowledge but also gives undoubted certainty.

Thus, Reid accepts memory as an original but unaccountable faculty like perception and consciousness. It is a source of our knowledge of things past, of duration and of personal identity, though we cannot explain how it operates or produces knowledge except that we are so made.

Reid is very critical of the representative account of memory as given by Hume. Writing about memory, Hume says, that we find by experience that, when any impression has been present with the mind, it again makes its appearance there as an idea; and this it may do after two different ways, either when in its new appearance it retains a considerable degree of its first vivacity and is somewhat intermediate betwixt an impression and an idea, or when it entirely loses that vivacity, and is a perfect idea. The faculty by which we repeat our impressions in the first manner is called the memory, and the other the imagination.

Reid's initial objection to such an account of memory is that the 'experience' which makes us aware of the appearance of idea is nothing but memory itself—but memory as commonly accepted. By memory Hume means present idea but this depends upon memory as commonly accepted. In other words, unless we remember clearly the first impression, experiencing its second or third recurrence with varying degrees of strength and vivacity is not possible.

Moreover, impressions are momentary and fleeting. To say that they make the second or the third appearance is to grant them the continued existence which is not possible.

The main difficulty with representative account of memory is that it treats only ideas as immediate objects of thought and this invariably leads to scepticism regarding memory; from our having a certain idea presently in our mind, it is impossible to conclude that an event really happened some years ago. In Reid's own words:

"There is the same need of arguments to prove that the ideas of memory are pictures of things that really did happen as that the ideas of sense are pictures of external objects which now exist. In both cases it will be impossible to find any argument that has real weight. So that this hypothesis leads us to absolute scepticism with regard to those things which we most distinctly remember, no less than with regard to the external objects of sense".[16]

To summarise Reid's treatment of the problem of memory: He treats memory as an immediate act, involving no inference, it has as its object the event or situation remembered; no reason can be given to establish conclusively the reliability of any act of remembering except that it is so. He totally denies the intervention of images; but he does not openly advocate a realistic view that memory is a simple act of apprehending the past event as very much like perception which is an act of apprehending a present fact.[17] Woozley's argument that this would make all memory-beliefs infallible is not tenable. Memory beliefs are presentative and yet at times their validity is suspect as is the case with perception.

Views of Psychologists

The psychologists too have considered memory as an important phenomenon. It is closely associated with learning, which is the key process in human behaviour. It pervades everything we do and think. We are as it were immersed in a world which demands constant learning. Learning and remembering what is learnt enable people to participate fully in the life of their society. The tremendous achievements of human kind are made possible by verbal learning or the input of information, memory or storage of information and retrieval or output of information. In fact, since we are talking animals, learning and memory of verbal materials are a key to our existence. Hence psychologists have considered it as one of the major jobs of psychology to understand this human species-specific activity.

As Boring, Langfeld and Weld have mentioned the very process of human thinking is closely connnected with recollecting and imagining. As a result, recollecting and imagining are referred to as thinking. But thinking is a very complicated process and not just a matter of reviving from the storage or creating images. These are rather two important tools for thinking.

Recollection is a process by which events and situations from the past are recreated by the individual and recognised by him as coming from his past. Recollection thus emphasises recognition. It primarily refers to visual senses but even other sense departments may be involved.

Even for describing the recollected events, we use the same terms as used for describing the perceived events or objects — colour, shape, sound, warmth etc. It is really difficult to suggest a criterion that can clearly distinguish perceptions from recollections. The world of perception is a complex but unitary whole and all the items of experience make up a consistent systematic whole. Recollection and imagination make up the experience that comes into our life without fitting the basic perceptual pattern. We are recollecting when what we experience fits into a past perceptual system, is dated and placed in relation to past places and events.

With the help of various experiments, psychologists have tried to determine the reliability of recollections. Advance instructions that the subject has to recall what he is perceiving tend to decrease (but not eliminate) the errors in recollection. Under the pressure of cross-examination many more errors are committed than what they would be otherwise. Recollection is also affected by the lapse of time. Many times recollection of an event is a result of many previous rehearsals.

Recollection admits of various kinds. Accurate recollection of the same object or event does not necessarily always take the same form. One type of difference is according to sense department used. The other difference is between verbal recollection and one in terms of concrete imagery. But most persons use all the types on different occasions. The most important recollections for civilised adults are general and abstract, not concrete and objective and hence imagery makes very little difference in human life. The verbal recollection is the most efficient, though not always perfectly accurate.

Even Norman Munn maintains that without memory, learning is impossible. Memory differs in degree; but it is doubtful if anything once learnt is completely forgotten. Memory for something may be complete, it may be partial or it may be even negligible.

As Munn maintains, memory essentially involves the making of an impression by an experience, the retention of some record of this impression and the re-entry of this record into consciousness as recall and recognition. But in its most general sense it is retaining. It is mediated by the modifications of neurons which are referred to as memory traces.

Before language develops, memory is evidenced by reproduction of a motor performance, relearning a habit quickly and delayed reactions. Verbal recall is also studied in various ways. Its study with the help of memorization of various items, recall of narratives, reproduction of forms, testimony shows that our memory may be erroneous and distorted or extremely accurate. Narratives and testimony may contain errors but memory containing eidetic imagery may be absolutely accurate and trustworthy.

Even a small part of the former stimulating situation may elicit the recall of the whole situation. The procedures which help fast learning are also conducive to good retention. Distributed learning and recitation are two such procedures.

More or less the same features of memory are also noted by Morgan and King when they speak of memory-store model[18]. The psychologists, thus treat memory as an important kind of cognitive activity. Its close association with learning shows that like learning, it also pervades entire human behaviour. The tremendous progress which human beings have made is made possible by their verbal learning, but an equally important contributory factor is that the humans have an access to this knowledge through memory. The psychologists have also rightly emphasised the close connection between perception and memory making any clear-cut distinction between recollections and perceptions really difficult. They have admitted recollections as having various degrees of reliability. They have hinted at the fact that imagery after all does not play a very important role in memory.

Summary

Even in Western thought memory is looked upon as representational in nature whereby the past can be approached only through images or impressions; or it is treated as presentational in nature implying that past is directly presented to us as a matter of perception. It is also possible to come across views which admit the representational character of memory but still consider imagery not particularly important or indispensable. Thus Russell considers memory as a kind of mirroring or a kind of intuitive knowledge—images may be there but they do not constitute the essence of memory. Even according to Ayer, images play only an auxiliary role. We, as it were, see the original through the images. He even goes to the extent of saying that better one's memory functions, more readily one approaches the past without intervening images.

There appears to be a general agreement that memory gives the reliable and trustworthy knowledge of past. The reliability itself admits of various degrees which are determined by various factors, but it is undeniably true that memory introduces us to knowledge in one of its forms — it is a revelation of thing through the mist of intervening time. Some thinkers like Alexander and Stout accept is as a kind of immediate and non-inferential knowledge. Again, almost all thinkers emphasise that it is not just the knowledge of past, but it is the knowledge of one's own past; this kind of knowledge is justified by the character of actual present experience. Reid treats memory as a kind of separate faculty belonging to us (alongwith many other faculties) but he criticises and rejects Hume's view of it as a representative faculty. His position is very akin to the realistic view that memory is an act of simple apprehension of past, very much like perception which is an act of simple apprehension of present.

A general review of the Western thinkers' views on memory also makes us aware of various other cognitive functions performed by memory (in addition to giving us the knowledge of past and then too, one's own past). A single memory is incomplete and it throws out feelers to other aspects of a thing and to other things and our memory is built by other memories through their internal coherence and continuity. Thus memory-knowledge is a knowledge of composite whole. Ayer points out another function of memory. According to him, our knowledge of the causal direction of events is determined by our reliance on memory. We believe that we can causally influence the future events as human action is essentially forward-moving, but we cannot affect the course of past events, because the past events are already known to exist. It is our memory which helps us to take note of what has happened.

Memory-knowledge also makes us aware of the continuity between the past event and the present remembrance and it is a continuity in the consciousness of the same person. Remembrance creates the awareness of the conviction of our own existence. In other words, it is a source of our knowledge of personal identity. And it does not merely give knowledge; it gives undoubted certainty.

Lastly, our acquisition of the knowledge of the concept of duration is also due to memory.

In fact, memory is an essential element in human thinking. Therefore, not only the past but even future will come to naught if memory is not accepted as valid or as a source of valid knowledge.

Nature of Memory—Part II (Views of Indian thinkers)

Even in India, the problem of memory has attracted the attention of various thinkers. It has been treated on both the psychological level—as a mental event produced by certain determinants and connected with certain other facts like recognition, retention, forgetfulness etc. — and on the philosophical level — as a process connected with apprehension, as the only process taking us into the past and as giving the knowledge of past. Considered philosophically, memory is analysed in different ways — views ranging from memory as a kind of perception to memory as a phenomenon where a present momentary idea just happens to be associated with some past momentary idea.

We are naturally more interested in examining the claim of memory as a means of valid knowledge of the past. Still it is worth our while to go through different accounts of memory as given by different thinkers.

According to Gautama, the self which is a permanent substance endowed with knowledge can recall an object of its past experience. According to Vātsyāyana, recollection is recalling and recognising an object perceived in the past by the same self. One and the same self perceived the object in the past, remembers it at present, and recognizes it as an object of its past experience. Recollection appears in the form, "I have known it before". Vātysāyana's account of memory attributes certain features to memory. Memory presupposes a past apprehension of an object. It also presupposes an impression produced by the past apprehension. The awakening (udbodhana) of impressions due to some excitants is also necessary for the operation of memory. A full account of recollection also implies recognition of the remembered object as perceived in the past. This object is referred to a particular time in the past. The phenomenon of recollection presupposes identity of the self. Or else, one person's perception will be another person's recollection. The self has the essential nature of knowing the past, present and future. (trikālavyāpini jñānaśaktireva jñasvābhāvyam। — Nyāyavārtikatātparyatīkā by Vācaspatimiśra; p. 403)[19]

Keśavamiśra also distinguishes cognition (Buddhi) into two— apprehension (anubhava) and remembrance (smaraṇa). Remembrance, again is of two kinds—true and false. In the waking state, we have both these kinds of remembrance. In dream on the other hand all cognition without exception is remembrance and false, because there the cognition 'this' arises in the place of 'that' due to some defect—smaraṇamapi yathārthamayathārtham ceti dvividham । Tadubhayam jāgare । svapne tu sarvameva jñānam smaraṇamayathārtham ca । Doṣavaśena taditi sthāna idamityudayāt ।[20]

Keśavamiśra himself does not define smṛti. Generally the Naiyāyikas understand smṛti as jñātaviṣayam jñānam—it is a cognition referring to something which had been already known before (under different circumstances). It may be noted that this definition applies to recognition (pratyabhijñā) as well.

Praśastapāda's Views

Praśastapāda divides cognition into two kinds—Vidyā or valid knowledge and avidyā, i.e. invalid knowledge. Vidyā is also accepted as of four kinds of which smṛti or memory is one. (others are pratyakṣa, i.e. perception, anumāna, i.e. inference and ārṣa, i.e. extraordinary knowledge available to the sages).

Praśastapādā defines smṛti as:

> Liṅgadarśanecchānusmaraṇādyapekṣādātmamanasoḥ saṁyogaviśeṣāt paṭvābhyāsādarapratyayajanitācch saṁskārād dṛṣṭaśṛtānubhūteṣvartheṣu Śeṣānuvyavasāyecchānusmaraṇadveṣaheturatītaviṣayā Smṛtiriti |[21]

The definition is very exhaustive as it includes various aspects of smṛti — factors which arouse samṛti, objects of smṛti and effects of smṛti. Thus smṛti is said to be caused by a special kind of contact between mind and soul which is aided by the perception of suggestive sign (liṅga-darśana), will to recall (icchā), thinking of associated ideas (anusmaraṇa) etc. According to Shreedhara, the word 'ādi' (translated as 'etc') refers to the conditions of recall such as praṇidhāna etc. mentioned by Gautama in Nyāya-Sūtra.

Gautama mentions the following conditions as causing remembrance (these are also implicitly accepted by Praśastapāda in his definition of smṛti): praṇidhāna or the fixation of mind on the object or on the suggestive signs which have the power of reviving the impression of the object; nibandha or context; abhyāsa or repetition which produces intense impression; liṅga or suggestive signs which are associated with the object in the experience; lakṣaṇa or distinguishing features which remind us of the objects which possess these features; sādṛśya or similarity; ownership or parigraha due to which owner reminds us of the owned and vice versa; āśraya or supporter which reminds us of the supported; the same is true of āśrita or supported; any other relationship not mentioned so far; ānantarya or immediate sequence in which one preceding item reminds another immediately succeeding it; viyoga or separation which generally involves the experience of sorrow reminding one of the object of sorrow; ekakārya or the identity of function where the factors or individuals acting together to produce an effect remind us of one another; virodha or antagonism in which the objects well-known as being antagonistic remind us of one another; atiśaya or excess reminds us of what brings it about; prāpti or attainment reminds us of the source of attainment; vyavadhāna or concealment in which what conceals an object reminds us of what is concealed; sukha-duḥkha or pleasure and pain remind us of their causes and also of each other; icchā-dveṣa or desire and aversion remind us of the objects exciting them; bhaya (fear), rāga (affection), arthitva (need), kriyā (action) are some of the remaining factors mentioned by Gautama; dharma (merit) and adharma (demerit) are factors involved in the extraordinary recollections from past lives.

Gautama's list is by no means exhaustive; its value is more suggestive than enumerative in nature. Praśastapāda seems to implicitely accept all these factors though explicitely he mentions only liṅgadarśana, icchā and anusmarana.

Like these three aiding the special contact between mind and soul, another instrumental cause of smṛti is impressions. Praśastapāda qualifies these impressions as patvābhyāsādarapratyayajanitāt. Just any impression cannot produce recall. The impressions produced by intense and distinct experience, repeated experience and vivid experience form the instrumental cause of smṛti. Intense perception of an object produces deep and long lasting impression. Thus a person who has never seen a serpent moving freely before retains such an impression for a long time afterwards if he happens to see one in the forest. However Śrīdhara interprets patupratyaye to mean sphuṭatarapratyaya or intense as well as distinct cognition because according to him mere intense cognition may not always produce lasting impressions. If we walk on grass barefooted, we may have intense factual cognition but still it may not produce vivid impressions as it lacks distinctness. Repeated cognition or abhyāsa is also equally important. A chapter of the Veda read first time may fail to produce any impression, but when the same is repeated frequently, its distinct perception is thus repeated and it produces deep impression. Cognition with interest (ādarpūrvakagrahaṇam) is also another condition of lasting impressions. This is the reason why an awe-inspiring or marvellous object is always remembered even when it is seen only once. The object evokes great interest and sustains single-minded attention; therefore a deep and vivid impression is formed.

Memory, according to Praśastapāda is of the objects seen, objects known through testimony and objects known through inference. In the next place, the definition of memory also mentions the functions of memory. Memory causes śeṣānuvyavasāya, i.e. anumiti or inferential knowledge (remembering vyāpti is instrumental for inferential knowledge). Memory also produces desire for object because we remember objects as giving pleasure in the past; it is also a cause of subsequent memory or anusmaraṇa. Remembering one word from a sentence leads to the memory of a subsequent word from the same sentence. Memory of an object that has caused pain in the past produces aversion towards that object.

Lastly, Praśastapāda mentions a feature of memory which has bearing on the status of memory as a pramāṇa. It is that memory is atītavisayā i.e. the subject of which is past; "that was" is the form of smṛti; this form suggests the pastness and being previously experienced of the object :

> Tadityeva smṛterākārah tatra cārthasyātītatvam
> Pūrvānubhūtatvam pratīyata ityatītaviṣayā smṛtiḥ. ||[22]

Annam Bhaṭṭa

Even Annam Bhaṭṭa classifies knowledge into remembrance and apprehension. Both are further classified into true and false. He defines smṛti as— Saṁskāramātrajam jñānam smṛtiriti. It is a knowledge born of a mental impression alone. This impression or saṁskāra is of the variety called Bhavanāsaṁskāra which is an operation born of anubhava and causing smṛti. It exists between the product smṛti and its cause, viz. anubhava. The insertion of the word mātra in the definition helps to exclude pratyabhijñā from its scope as pratyabhijñā is not born of impression alone. The impressions are generally gained through perception, but they can be gained through other sources as well. Smṛti properly speaking is general and comprehends all impressions. As Athalye and Bodas remark in their critical notes on Tarkasaṁgraha, remembrance or reminiscence is an act by which we endeavour to recall and re-unite former states of consciousness, and it is a kind of reasoning by which we ascend from a present consciousness to a former one.

Smṛti is of two kinds according to Annam Bhaṭṭa: true and false. The one arising from true apprehension is true and arising from false apprehension is false. Thus according to him the basis for the truth or falsity of apprehension (anubhava) is different from the basis for the truth or falsity of memory. In the case of memory the truth or falsity depends upon that of original apprehension or anubhava. The reason seems to be that memory is not directly connected with the external objects. There is possibly another supporting argument that remembrance is considerably removed in time as well as in space from the first apprehension; hence the criterion of prāmāṇya as applying to the apprehension (inference based upon actual verification of the external object) cannot apply to memory. But this is not a satisfactory criterion because even a true apprehension may result in false memory.

Jaina View

Jainas admit two kinds of means of valid knowledge — perceptual and non-perceptual. It is already noted that non-perceptual knowledge or parokṣajñāna (which is defined as cognition lacking immediacy and lucidity but which nonetheless is definitive and authentic) is further sub-divided into recollection, recognition, inductive reasoning, inference and verbal testimony.

Māṇikyanandi, a Jaina philosopher, defines recollection as a cognition in the form of 'that' which is produced by the revival of an impression.

(Saṁskārodbodhanibandhanā tadityākārā smṛtiḥ— Parīkṣāmukhasūtra-iii-3[23]

Even Hemachandra defines recollection as a cognition which has for its condition the stimulation of a memory-impression and which refers to its content by a form of the pronoun 'that': (Vāsanodbodhahetukā tadiyākārā smṛtiḥ — Pramānamīmāṁsā; I, 2.3)[24].

A memory-impression is what is deposited by past experience. Its stimulation means its being excited and brought to the surface of consciousness. Thus the emergence of recollection is necessarily conditioned by the stimulation and mere impression by itself cannot produce recollection. When, however, the requisite conditions such as the annihilation of obstructive veils, observation of similar objects and the like are operative to bring the impression to maturation, the recollection is produced. The word 'tadiyākārā' refers to the mode of communication of memory.

Even Prabhācandra defines recollection as a cognition in the form of 'that' due to the revival of an impression generated by the perception of an object on a previous occasion—the revival being due to the perception or thought of a cue. According to Bhaṭṭa Akalaṅka, if the past perception did not cognize itself, then the present recollection would be a novel knowledge and as a consequence it would cease to be recollection. But it is an already acquired knowledge devoid of novelty and therefore a reproduction of a past perception which cognized itself.

On the whole, the Jainas seem to be favourably inclined to accepting memory as an organ of knowledge since it is never found to be discrepant with fact which is further attested by successful activities (such as search for thing deposited by one's own self). It is possible to question such a status of memory. Hemacandra discusses various objections to accepting memory as an organ of knowledge and also refutes them. But it is more desirable to discuss these arguments and counter-arguments in the chapter 'Status of Memory' than in 'Nature of Memory'.

Bauddha View

Buddhist's views on memory follow from their theory of momentariness. According to the Buddhists so called identity is nothing but a continuous series of similar momentary things. Therefore the self is also nothing but a series of momentary cognitions. There is no separate permanent self behind the continuous series of momentary congnitions. The earlier cognition leaves an impression which modifies the succeeding cognition. These impressions are transferred from one cognition to another, and this constitutes the explanation of memory. Memory does not require any permanent self which retains impressions within itself and remembers the past cognition when the impressions are revived. Our cognitions form a series and a future member of the same series of cognitions remembers (due to carried-over impressions) a past momentary object perceived by a past member of the same series. Thus stream of momentary cognitions can account for memory as well.

It is obvious that such a doctrine of momentariness makes knowledge itself impossible; hence the question of there being any valid memory-knowledge does not arise. Moreover, on the Buddhist view, only indeterminate perception or the perception of an object in its uniqueness, unassociated with names and other determinations is valid. But since memory-cognition cannot be the result of indeterminate perception, it follows that on Buddhist view it would be invalid knowledge.

Sāṁkhya-Yoga

The Sāṁkhya defines recollection as the cognition of a past object or a cognition produced by an impression (Smṛtiratītajñānam — SSV, ii, 33 and Smṛtiḥ saṁskārajanyam jñānam SPB ii, 33)[25]. It is the representative cognition of an object perceived in the past due to the resuscitation of an impression (SSV, iv, 21).

Even Yoga gives a similar account of recollection. In the fifth and sixth sūtra of Samādhipāda Patañjali speaks of five kinds of mental modifications, all of which may be with or without afflictions and smṛti or memory is one of them while means of valid knowledge (pramāṇa), error (viparyaya), (vikalpa) and sleep (nidrā) are the remaining four.

Vṛttayaḥ pañcatayyaḥ kliṣṭākliṣṭāḥ ||5||

Pramāṇaviparyayavikalpanidrāsmṛtayaḥ ||6||

Pātañjdayogadarśana.

In the eleventh sūtra, he defines smṛti as: Anubhūtaviṣayāsaṁpramoṣaḥ smṛtiḥ|| — Memory is a corresponding cognition arising in the citta—a cognition of an object apprehended before. It is nothing but arousal of the impressions of earlier apprehension. These may be aroused by the external circumstances similar to the original apprehension or by the intense desire to arouse one. The aroused impressions assume the form of mental modification of the nature of smṛti. Smṛti, thus, does not cognise anything in excess of the object of past apprehension.

A question is asked in this connection — Does mind remember a cognition or an object? According to Vyāsa recollection cognises both a cognition and an object. A cognition is coloured by its object. Consciousness is common to all cognitions, but they are distinguished from one another by their objects which colour them. Such cognitions leave their impressions of a similar nature. When such an impression is revived, it produces a recollection of past cognition and its object.

Sūtra No. 9 of Kaivalyapāda refers to some unique functions of smṛti. The sūtra reads as:

Jātideśakālavyavahitāmapyānantaryam smṛti — saṃskārayorekarūpatvāt ||9||— Kaivalyapāda— Pātañjalayogadarśana.

The Sūtra means that — 'The original impressions and the revived and expressed tendencies (relevant to this birth) are separated by many births in different places and at different times; yet the impressions of those tendencies only (and then also of those which are relevant now) are revived because impressions and revived tendencies are of the identical nature.'

The enjoyment or experience (bhoga) of jīvātmā depends upon the suitable actions on the part of motor-organs and cognitive organs; the actions, in their turn, are determined by the revival of the relevant knowledge of objects as stored in buddhi; but the revival of knowledge is itself due to the revival of the desires. Only those desires are revived from their original impressions which are relevant to the present enjoyment of jīvātmā. The implicit impressions and explicit desires are of identical nature. Memory, then, is instrumental in reviving the impressions which contain the unexpressed seeds of desires, knowledge and actions.

Pārthasārathi Miśra defines recollection as a cognition that cognizes an object apprehended before — that never cognizes an unapprehend object. Prābhākaras distinguish knowledge into valid and invalid. Of these the first is called anubhūti and the second smṛti, i.e. memory which is different from apprehension. (Pramāṇam anubhūtiḥ na ca smṛteh prāmāṇyāpattiriti darśayati, sā smrteranyā—Indian Epistemology by Jwala Prasad; Part IV, p. 281). It is invalid because it is produced entirely by the impressions left by a previous cognition.

Advaita Vedānta View

As already noted, according to Advaita Vedānta the entire field of empirical knowledge manifesting itself in different forms is wrapped in the veil of ignorance. The real nature of things is never known to us. So empirical knowledge pertains to the domain of ignorance and it only distorts (and does not reveal) the real.

The means of right knowledge are also therefore based upon ignorance. Of course we do not find a systematic treatment of the means of knowledge in any of Śaṅkara's works. But he seems to regard that within the confines of phenomenal existence, we must accept the distinction between right cognition and error. He regards dreams as memory or recollections. (Smṛtireṣā yatsvapnadarśanam — S.B., ii, 2, 29)[26]. In a sleeping person's mind, only impressions persist which produce dreams. They are false because they are tainted by sleep.

Vācaspati Miśra defines recollection as a cognition which is produced by an impression only. It is different from apprehension consisting of perception, inference, testimony, comparison, presumption and non-apprehension. According to Prakāśānanda, the past cognition produces an impression which causes recollection; even recollection cognises an object only and not the past cognition (because even past cognition cognized its object only and not itself). Mādhavācārya Vidyāraṇya regards recollection as a reproduction of an object exactly as it was apprehended in the past; the reproduction depends upon the mere revival of the impression of the past apprehension. It cannot be created, destroyed or altered at will. In Vedāntaparibhāṣā Dharmarāja Adhvarin mentions both the views which maintain that memory is invalid knowledge and that memory is valid knowledge, implying that memory can be admitted as valid knowledge. Thus he states: Tatra smṛtivyāvṛtam pramātvam anadhigatābādhitārthaviṣayakajñānatvam, smṛtisādhāraṇam tu abādhitārthaviṣayakajñānatvam I[27]. Here, the nature of such valid knowledge, as excludes recollection, consists in being cognition having for content an entity that is not already known and is not sublated; whereas, that (nature of valid knowledge) which is common to recollection consists in being cognition having for content an unsublated entity. Thus prāmāṇya is purposely defined in two ways so as to accommodate or reject the claim of memory for being valid knowledge. P.K. Sundaram, while commenting on these two definitions of pramātva remarks that, that memory is valid is not the same as to say that memory is an independent source of knowledge. He further holds that memory does not reveal anything that is not revealed by anything else. It may be noted in this context that though Sundaram bases his reasoning on Dharmarāja's two definitions of pramā, Dharmarāja himself does not make any distinction between memory as valid knowledge and memory as a source of valid knowledge.

On the whole, Advaitins seem to accept the representational nature of memory as arising from residual impressions. Hence they do not find a need to accept it as independent knowledge, though it would be more proper, to say that they are rather indifferent to whole problem and unwilling to take sides.

Viśiṣṭādvaita

The followers of Rāmānujācarya have discussed the problem of memory in detail. Generally, they seem to accept the validity of memory without accepting it as a separate means of valid knowledge. According to Meghanādāri, one of the characteristics of pramāṇa is actually absent in memory and yet he argues that the memory cannot be divested of the claim to validity. He defines pramāṇa as the knowledge that determines the nature of objects without depending on the other sources of knowledge such as memory —

> Tatrānyapramāṇānapekṣamarthaparicchedakam jñānam pramāṇam, arthaparicchede'nyapramānāsāpekṣasmṛtāvativyāptiparihāre' nyapramāṇānapekṣamiti![28].

Thus the phrase "not depending upon other sources of knowledge" aims at obliterating the possibility of making the definition too wide as memory obviously depends upon anubhūti or apprehension for determining the nature of object. But he further argues that memory, being spontaneous does not depend upon anything else for its self-manifestation. It is true, no doubt that the revelation of objects in memory depends upon the fact of their having been perceived before, but the functioning of memory is undoubtedly spontaneous — Svasphuraṇe pramāṇāntarasāpekṣatvābhāvāt viṣayasphuraṇa eva hi smṛteḥ pūrvānubhūtabhāvāpekṣā ।[29]. Meghanādāri does not accept the argument that memory may be partly valid in so far as its own functioning is concerned, but it is also partly invalid so far as the revelation of the objects is concerned (because it depends upon previous perception, and therefore is not a spontaneous manifestation of objects). According to him the spontaneous manifestation of memory-cognition is also at the same time the revelation of the object remembered, the implication being that revelation of knowledge implies the revelation of objects also— Jñānasphūrtivadviṣayasyāpi sphūrtiḥ ।[30].

Veṅkaṭanātha (or Vedāntadeśika) gives the same definition of recollection as Prabhākara, Vācaspati Miśra and others give — Saṁskāramātrajam jñānam smṛtiḥ iti tallakṣaṇam ।[31]. He observes that a recollection cognises that particular object, the apprehension of which produces it. In other words, the perception (or any other apprehension) of an object produces recollection and the recollection cognises that object which was known by perception in the past — smṛteḥ: anubhūtavyaktiniyataviṣayatvam ।[32].

He is strongly in favour of accepting correct memory as a source of valid knowledge. He declares in Nyāyapariśuddhi — Smṛtimātrāpramāṇatvam na yuktamiti vakṣyate I Abādhitasmṛterloke pramānatvaparigrahat I[33]. It is improper to say that memory as such is invalid because memory which is not contradicted (which is a knowledge of a thing as it is and which satisfies the practical interests of life—an accepted criterion of validity by Veṅkatanātha — (yathāvasthitavyavahārānuguṇam jñānam prameti) is accepted as valid in this world. Since valid knowledge is that which produces behaviour leading to an experience of things as they are, memory is naturally included in it, and is also treated as a source of valid knowledge. but though he treats it as a source of valid knowledge, it is not to be classed as an independent source of knowledge. It is to be included within the pramāṇa or a source of valid knowledge which is responsible for memory (e.g. perception). It is thus but a mode of perception.

Dvaita Vedānta View

Madhvā brings memory under Pratyakṣa. He considers it as a direct perception by mind. Thus it is said: Pratyakṣam saptavidham I Sākṣiṣaḍindriyabhedena I Mānasapratyakṣajā smṛtiḥ I[34] Perception is of seven kinds; it is due to the distinct operations of six sense organs and a special sense organ acting as an instrument of intuitive perception, i.e. sākṣī, smṛti is born of direct perception by mind. In it, the mind is in contact with the past. The saṁskāras provide this contact. The possibility of thus reaching into the past is established by the evidence of Yogic perception of past and future. There is nothing inconceivable about it.

Memory, is thus accepted as a form of and organ of valid knowledge concerning past. This is made possible by the definition of pramāṇa as yathārtha. The Nyāya school, the Prābhākara Bhāṭṭa school and the Advaita school purposely define pramāṇa is such a way as to exclude memory from its scope. Their definition of pramāṇa is — Anadhigatārthagantṛ Pramāṇam - that alone is a source of valid knowledge which acquaints us with the object not acquired (i.e. apprehended) before. In short, novelty is insisted upon as a feature of validity. It is argued that memory does not tell us anything new as it is simply the reproduction of past experience (In this respect, the difference between the definitions of smṛti given by the above mentioned schools and one given by Madhvācārya is also worth noting. The others emphasise such features of memory as saṁskārajanyā or born of previous impressions, tadityākārāor of the form of 'that', jñātavisayā or the object of which is known before and the like; for Madhvācārya, its being mānasapratyakṣajā or born of direct mental perception is important). Hence they do not accept memory as source of a valid knowledge. But according to Madhvācārya pramāṇa is that which has a capacity to reveal the nature of an object as it really is. Since memory has this capacity, it is a pramāṇa. (It can recall the fact that the particular object was in such and such a condition at such and such a time). He regards the insistence on novelty as unnecessary and unjustified restriction on the scope of pramāṇas.

But even if the demand for novelty were to be insisted upon, memory can be shown as satisfying that condition too. If the previous experience presents the object as 'now present', recollection presents its object, "as past". This new feature belongs to memory-knowledge alone and not to previous experience.

In making memory a kind of perceptual cognition, the dvaitins have accepted it as an immediate and direct knowledge.

Madhvācārya insists that the validity of memory is not inferential as generally believed, because in that case even the perception of an object like a jar can be treated as an inference from kārya to a kāraṇa: Sākṣātkāreṇa kāryeṇa karmakārakatayā ghaṭādyanumānam I[35]. Since from the perceived effect, the instrumental cause is inferred, the existence of a jar too will be an inference (from the perceived ghatājñān)

He does not accept another argument also that memory may be dispensed with and the past may be known by inference from the retention of the impressions of the past experience or from its revival as an image. Such an inference itself would involve memory of what happened in the past which is retained as an impression.

Thus, the dvaita view of the nature of memory is that it is a source and form of valid knowledge which cannot be reduced to any other form. It is also svataḥpramāṇa and not depending on other factors for its validity. It is an immediate and direct perception of the past by mind. Such a position is an advance over the view of Jainas who accept it as a source of valid knowledge but still classify it as a kind of mediate knowledge or parokṣa-jñāna. It is more consistent than Nyāya view which admits the possibility of a true memory-cognition but refuses to accept memory as a source of valid knowledge. And this is maintained by them in spite of the fact that they understand 'knowledge' in the widest possible sense, i.e. any awareness or consciousness of an object. His views come very close to the views of Russell who claims that "we often remember what we have seen or heard or had otherwise presented to our senses and in such cases, we are still immediately aware of what we remember, in spite of the fact that it appears as past and not as present[36].

Modern Developments

From amongst the modern thinkers, the views of Acārya Jwālā Prasāda on the nature of knowledge in general and memory in particular are worth mentioning. He accepts knowledge as that action in which the grasping of the nature of an object takes place. The intellect or Buddhi is that faculty of consciousness by means of which the nature of an object is grasped. This instrument of knowledge i.e. Buddhi has two forms: Experience and memory. The intellect which has its basis in the impressions of previous experience is Memory. Acārya Jwālā Prasāda does not accept memory as one of the means of valid knowledge which include perception, direct knowledge and reasoning. Memory, in short, is a faculty of revival of knowledge in consciousness.

In this context, Jwālā Prasāda makes a very important point. Though he accepts only experience, i.e. anubhava as producing valid knowledge, he also admits that knowledge obtained from experience is usually mixed with memory. There is an element of memory in perception, direct knowledge and also reasoning. Even when the object is perceived for the first time, the perception must still be aided by the memory of names, classes, qualities etc.

He also admits that valid knowledge is that in experience or in memory which accords with the nature of object. Not only is the meaning of validity same in experience and in memory, but the kinds of valid knowledge in experience and memory also are same and so also is the proof of validity of knowledge in experience and memory.

Thus valid knowledge (in experience as well as in memory) is either with regard to existence (bhāvātmakam) or non-existence (abhāvātmakam); for example, it can be a valid knowledge of an object that exists or valid knowledge of an object that does not exist. Similarly in the case of memory, there is valid knowledge with regard to existence when there is revival of an object in memory exactly corresponding to that as perceived previously, while there is valid knowledge with regard to non-existence when there is revival in memory of the non-existence of an object which was not perceived previously.

The validity of knowledge in experience is proved by its steadiness in one's own mind and its correspondence to the knowledge of others. In other words, true knowledge remains fairly steady in the mind and its validity is established by its being confirmed by other minds. Even the validity of knowledge in memory is proved in the same way. Thus when there is steadiness of knowledge in memory in one's own mind and the knowledge corresponds with that of others, it is valid. The contrary of that is its invalidity.

Thus the trend is to treat memory as on par with experience both are the forms of intellect, both can result in valid as well as invalid knowledge, both admit of same kinds of valid knowledge and both depend upon same conditions for proving their validity.

Conclusion

On analysing, different views on memory as expressed by different Indian Thinkers, we note that memory is treated as purely representatational in nature by some thinkers and as presentational or of the nature of perception by certain others. Those treating it as representational exphasise the features such as 'born of impressions', 'lacking in novelty' 'of the form of "that".' Among the representationists, such thinkers as Jainas accept it as a kind of valid knowledge, while others like Naiyāyikas and Mīmāṃmsakas treat it as invalid. The presentationists like Veṅkaṭanātha and Madhvācārya accept it as a kind of valid knowledge. The later thinkers have noted many such features of correct memory which justify its claim for being a valid knowledge and also a source of valid knowledge. Some of these features are — it is never discrepant with facts, it leads to successful activity, it is spontaneous in its own manifestation as well as that of its objects, its pastness itself constitutes its novelty, steadiness in our mind and its correspondence with the knowledge in other minds are also noteworthy. Thus there is the increasing awareness that memory-cognition can no longer be discarded as invalid cognition. A modern thinker like Acārya Jwālā Prasāda even treats it as on par with apprehension or anubhava. Accepting it as an independent source of its own peculiar knowledge is just one step ahead in the same direction but the fact remains that he does not take it.

The analysis of the essential nature and various features of memory raises certain important questions — if memory- cognition is such an important part of our cognition, what are the arguments against accepting it as a kind of valid knowledge? Is it possible to challenge and refute these objections? What has been and can be said in favour of memory as pramā and pramāṇa? Where does this discussion ultimately leave us? Such and allied questions are discussed in the next chapter, viz. 'Status of Memory'.

References

1. Essay concerning Human Understanding, p. 79.
2. Space, Time and Deity, by Samuel Alexander, Vol. I, p. 113.
3. Memory Knowledge in PAS, Supp. Vol. 15, 1936, 24.
4. Human Knowledge, pp. 440-441.
5. Problems of Philosophy, Chapter 11, p. 66.
6. Problems of Philosophy, Chapter 11, p. 67.
7. The Analysis of Mind, Lecture IX. p.
8. Space, Time and Deity by Samuel Alexander, Mental Space- Time, Book I, Chapter IV, p. 113.
9. The Problem of Knowledge by A.J. Ayer, Chapter IV 'Memory', p. 139.
10. The Principles of Psychology by William James, Vol. II, Chapter XVIII, p. 287.
11. The Principles of Psychology by William James, Vol. I, Chapter XVI, p. 650.
12. Studies in Philosophy and Psychology — Paper VIII, In What Way is Memory-knowledge Immediate? p. 166.
13. Studies in Philosophy and Psychology — Paper VIII, In What Way is Memory-knowledge Immediate? p. 175.
14. Ibid, p. 176.
15. Essay III — of Memory — Chapter I, pp. 195-196, Essays on the Intellectual Powers of Man.
16. Essays on the Intellectual Powers of Man — Essay III—Of Memory, p. 225.
17. Introduction to Reid's Essays on Intellectual Powers of Man, p. xxvi.
18. Appendix A.
19. Indian Psychology, Vol. I, Jadunath Sinha, p. 377.
20. The Tarkabhāṣa of Keśavamiśra, ed. by A.B. Gajendragadkar & R.D. Karmarkar, p. 94.
21. Praśastapādabhaṣya, edited by V.P. Dvivedin, p. 259.
22. Praśastapādabhāṣya, edited by Durgadhara Jha, p.
23. Indian Psychology by Jadunath Sinha Cognition, Vol. 1, Chapter XX, p. 377.
24. 'Jaina Philosophy' by Mohan Lal Mehta, p.
25. Indian Psychology by J.N. Sinha, p. 378.
26. Ibid, p. 379.
27. Vedantaparibhaṣha by Dharmarāja Adhvarin, ed. by S.S. Sūryanārāyaṇa Sāstrī, p. 3.

28. Nayadyumaṇi — quoted by S.N. Dasgupta, History of Indian Philosophy, Vol. III, p. 239.
29. Nayadyumaṇi — quoted by S.N. Dasgupta, A History of Indian Philosophy, Vol. III, p. 215.
30. Nayadyumaṇi—quoted by Dasgupta, A History of Indian Philosophy, Vol. III, p. 125.
31. Nyāya-pariśuddhi, Vedānta Deśika, p. 171.
32. Quoted by J.N. Sinha, Indian Psychology, p, 380.
33. Philosophy of Sri Madhvācarya (Rev. Edn.), B.N.K. Sharma, p. 139.
34. Philosophy of Sri Madhvācārya, by B.N.K. Sharma, Chapter XVI, p. 93.
35. Ibid, p. 93.
36. Problems of Philosophy, p. 76.

Chapter V

Status of Memory

Arguments Against the Validity of Memory

The analysis of memory done uptill now shows that the contribution of memory to knowledge is immense. Still the question of its status as pramā and as pramāṇa is highly controversial, a matter of hot dispute. The Naiyāyikas, Mīmāṃsakas and Advaitins in India and the sceptics in the West are very much opposed to the admission of memory-knowledge as valid. The Jainas, Dvaitins and most of the Viśiṣṭādvaitins admit its claim as valid knowledge. The Dvaitins and some Viśiṣṭādvaitins also accept it as a pramāṇa in its own right. Therefore, before we arrive at any definite conclusion regarding the status of memory, it is worth our while to go through various arguments and counter arguments both against and in favour of the validity of memory- knowledge.

The main arguments against the validity of memory are based upon the peculiar definitions of validity which cannot be satisfied by memory or are at least believed to be so. Thus validity is variously defined in terms of direct apprehension (anubhavatva), correspondence (yāthārthya), novelty (anadhigatatva) independence from other means of valid knowledge (anyapramāṇānapekṣatva), ability to serve useful purpose (saphalatvam) etc. and then an attempt is made to show that memory does not possess these features and is invalid on that account. In fact all these arguments commit the fallacy of petitio principii, as they first decide to put memory out of the scope of pramana and then define pramana. This is begging question. These, as well as other arguments against memory will now be discussed and examined in detail before we discuss arguments made in favour of memory as a kind of valid knowledge.

The most important argument made by the Naiyāyikas against the validity of memory-knowledge is that it is different from direct apprehension (anubhava). Valid knowledge, according to them is tattvānubhūti (direct apprehension of a thing's tattva, i.e. this-ness or that-ness) or yathārthānubhava (direct apprehension of an object as it really is). Since memory is not anubhava or anubhūti, i.e. direct apprehension, it cannot be valid cognition.

It is obvious that the Naiyāyikas purposely define pramā in terms of anubhava or anubhūti in order to exclude memory from the category of valid knowledge. Apart from the fact that there is nothing so very special about anubhava that it alone should constitute valid knowledge, we may also note two very important points made by Shrī Harsha in his Khaṇḍanakhaṇḍakhādya[1]. These are-firstly, the notion of anubhava or anubhūti itself is not very clear in its meaning and secondly, a total separation of anubhava and smṛti is not at all possible because many instances of anubhava seem to involve remembrance. We may go further and maintain that some instances of memory have such an immediacy, spontaneity and liveliness that they seem to involve anubhava, i.e. direct apprehension.

As Shrī Harsha points out, Anubhūti or Anubhava cannot be regarded as a sub-class of knowledge (jñāna) because determining the differentiation of such a sub-class is not possible. Nor can anubhūti be defined as knowledge oher than remembrance or as knowledge destitute of the character of remembrance. Such a definition supposes remembrance to be a more fundamental concept than anubhava so that anubhava can be defined in terms of remembrance. Moreover, it states what anubhava is not and not what it positively is. The most important objection to such a definition of anubhava is that recognition, i.e. pratyabhijñā which is accepted as a kind of valid knowledge is not at all other than remembrance. Recognition involves two different cognitions—one is of the nature of anubhava and the other is of the nature of remembrance. There two cognitions combined together give us the knowledge like, say for example, "This is the same jar as perceived in the past". The knowledge of the non-difference between the perceived jar and the remembered jar is impossible to have from pure perception or pure remembrance. Lastly, direct apprehension cannot be defined as knowledge which has a specific cause (karaṇa) coming into existence just before the knowledge. The reason is that even recognition is not produced merely by the specific cause of perception alone, i.e. sense-object contact and yet it is valid knowledge.

This discussion shows that the acceptance of anubhava as different from remembrance is full of contradictions. Its exact meaning and connotation cannot be decided. This discussion also emphasises that anubhava and smṛti cannot be totally separated from each other because in recognition, a kind of valid knowledge, we have both of them. It is therefore incorrect to argue that it is a universally acknowledged fact—viz., that on the ground of immediate consciousness we must admit that there is such a class-character as Direct Apprehension (anubhavatva) which excludes remembrance, but is present in all other cognition whether immediate (sensuous) or mediate (inferential and the like).

Śri Harsha further points out that even every tattvānubhūti, the direct apprehension of the object in its that-ness (true nature) is not valid knowledge (from our point of view, it means that therefore this cannot form genuine ground for rejecting validity to memory). There are occasions when cognitions happen to be right by chance. The cognition of a fruit falling off a palm-tree when crow sits on a branch is of this kind. If a person conceals five shells in his hand and the onlooker correctly cognises the number to be five, he has the direct apprehension of the object in its that-ness, but we would not call it valid knowledge. Even in the sphere of inference such examples of cognitions being right by chance can be had and we can show that they are not instances of pramā.

If yathārthānubhava or tattvānubhūti is not a proper explanation of pramā, then it implies that this at least cannot be a ground for rejecting memory as non-valid knowledge. We must, therefore turn to other arguments against memory.

Another argument generally put forward against memory as valid knowledge is that it does not fulfil the condition of correspondence (yāthārthya). The state or condition in which an object was first apprehended is no longer present at the time of its subsequent remembrance. As Jayanta puts it tadārūḍhasya vastunastadānīmasattvat.[2] Memory is non-valid cognition since its object is non-existent at the time of remembrance. Jayanta does not share the Mīmāṁsā view about the non-validity of memory as being due to its cognising what is already cognised (A view to be examined later). According to him what makes memory invalid is the fact that it does not arise out of objects themselves.

Na smṛterapramāṇatvam gṛhītagrāhitākṛtam |
Apitvanarthajanyatvam tadaprāmāṇyakāraṇam[3] ||

The contention here is that the objects which we remember once existed in the past but have now ceased to exist. So they are no longer real and there is no correspondence between the objects once perceived and their memory-images. Jayanta concludes that memory is not a valid knowledge as it is not based on only given datum, fails to give valid presentational experience and as such lacks yāthārthya.

Now, it is true that memory cannot be totally faithful to the experience and reproduce it exactly and hence lacks yāthārthya if that is how we interpret yāthārthya. But is this a proper interpretation of yāthārthya or correspondence? Is it proper to argue that knowledge is valid only when the knowledge-content exactly agrees with the nature of the object which is present then and there?

In the first place, let us point out that the concept of yāthārthya is interpreted variously by different thinkers. According to Nyāya, the subjective cognition of the relations and other characters of an object must correspond with the object as it is. But then such a criterion of truth cannot be applied to real general statements, hypothetical entities like atoms, electrons, other minds etc. which in themselves are unobservable. The demand for yāthārthya in this sense is a demand to treat whetever is not present now or cannot be experienced now as false, i.e. asat. As Shreedhara mentions in Nyāyakandali, in such a case even inferential knowledge as well as verbal testimony related to the object of the past experience or of future experience will be invalid (Ye twanarthajatvāt smṛterapramāṇyamāhuḥ teṣmatītānāgatavisayasyānumānasyāprāmāṇy1m syāditi duṣaṇam |[4]

The same point is also emphasised by Jayatīrtha in Nyāya-Sudhā (page 60) where he says : smaraṇakāle'rthasya tadavasthatvāthatvābhāvādayathārthyam smṛteriti . . . . Atītānāgataviṣayānumānāgamaprāmāṇyapracyatiḥ.

Atītādiviṣayasya tadānīmasattvat | . . . .

Tadavasthānivṛttyanivṛttyostūdāsinaiva (smṛtiḥ) | If it is argued that memory is invalid because at the time of remembrance the object does not exist in the same state, then even the inference and verbal testimony pertaining to past and future objects will be rendered invalid. The reason is that the object of past etc. is non- existent in them. As a matter of fact memory is indifferent to the retirement or non-retirement of the object from the same state (but these knowledges are accepted as valid despite the fact that their content does not exist at the present moment. There is no reason then why the anarthajanyatva (being produced in the absence of the object) should be considered as a fault in the case of memory alone sufficient to render it invalid.)

In fact, the demand for the actual presence of the object of cognition is similar to the demand for verifiability of every perceptual knowledge in order to make it meaningful, because the actual presence of an object is required for no other purpose than establishing correspondence. We know that the criterion of verifiability understood in its strict sense tends to make even perceptual knowledge meaningless and understood in its broad sense, it confers validity upon metaphysical statements as well. Similarly, yāthārthya understood in its strict sense tends to reject certain kinds of valid cognitions from the category of valid cognitions, but understood in its proper sense, it is seen to belong to memory as well and makes memory a kind of valid cognition.

The fact is that, even when memory cannot grasp its corresponding objects as present in the present time, it does grasp its objects existing at the time of their previous apprehension (if it were to cognise its objects as present in the present time, it would cease to be memory but would be perception). Hence, memory is not objectless (anartha). The very fact that it grasps the identity of the object as in the experience of 'that jar' means that it grasps the object having a past existence. This faithfulness to its object-content makes for the validity of memory and not the representation of the experience in toto. The existence of the object of memory in the same former condition is not merely impossible but it is also unessential. Memory merely recalls that a particular object was in such and such a condition at such and such a time. The object was originally apprehended in a particular space-time setting and also remembered in the same space-time setting, and this is a sufficient yāthārthya to determine the validity of memory. What is the present space-time setting of the object is irrelevant for the validity of memory. Yāthāthya which belongs to memory and renders it a valid cognition is expressed in a few but select meaningful words by Jayatīrtha: Syādidam yadanubhavānusāritvam yāthārthyamiti vadāmaḥ, arthānusāritvam tu tathetyuktam |[5]

It cannot also be said that the object of a previous knowledge cannot be the object of memory as it will change its state, because that will render all pramāṇas invalid to some extent as nothing can be an object of knowledge in all its entirety of conditions.

It also cannot be argued that memory should grasp the object unchanged. Memory is not concerned whether a thing has changed or not. Its task is only to cognise an entity as it was in the past. (Na hyanivṛttatadavastho'sāviti smṛtirālambate |

Kintu tadā'sau tādṛśa iti |[6]

An objection often raised against memory is that it does not have novelty, i.e. anadhigatatva. It is argued that the content of knowledge should be new or previously unacquired. The Mīmāṃsakas consider this to be an essential part of the validity of knowledge. They hold that it is not a function of a pramāṇa to make known what is already known. But since memory is only a reproduction of earlier apprehension or since it only represents the past experience, it lacks novelty and consequently validity.

There does not seem to be much force in this argument. It is very difficult to accept that no further knowledge of a once known object is possible or that knowledge is opposed to knowledge so that subsequent knowledge is debarred. Ultimately this condition will lead to an absurd position that absence of knowledge is a necessary condition of knowledge. So long as the conditions of knowledge are present, the knowledge will arise. Whether its object is new or not is immaterial to its validity. Otherwise the knowledge of permanent objects like the self or the sky will be impossible, because these have been already perceived by many.[7] It also cannot be said that the object of valid perception or inference should be such that it has not been perceived before by the present perceiver; for a person who knows the object already may seek to find it out and may perceive it but his perception would be invalid as it lacks anadhigatatva. Similarly an object perceived by the eye may be reperceived by the touch in which case the visual perception would be valid and the tactual perception would be invalid. It cannot be said that the newness of the temporal character constitutes the novelty in such perceptions. In that case, all memory-cognitions become automatically valid.

The importance given to novelty (anadhigatatva) poses a special problem in the case of persistent knowledge or continuous knowledge, i.e. dhārāvāhika jñāna. It is argued that if memory-knowledge is invalid because its object is already apprehended and therefore not new then even persistent knowledge in which the object once perceived is still under observation for some more moments continuously would be invalid. Of course, it is possible to hold that the object is new at every moment because of the addition of new temporal character. But it is really doubtful if every moment can be thus perceived separately; hence the argument against memory goes against persistent knowledge as well.

According to the Nyāya school, memory and persistent knowledge are still different (and the former is still invalid while the latter is valid) because in persistent knowledge, the knowledge of the subsequent moment is not caused by a reproduction of the knowledge of the earlier moment. It is caused by the same objective conditions which caused the earlier knowledge. (But if the conditions are exactly the same and temporal difference is unnoticeable, then wherein lies the newness of the object?) Memory, on the other hand is wholly a reproduction of a past knowledge. It falls back upon this past experience for is validity. Since it lacks novelty in this sense, it must be treated as invalid knowledge. D.M. Datta holds that this dependence of memory on past experience for its production and for determining its validity implies that memory abdicates its own claim in favour of its archetype. He further states that therefore, memory is not valid knowledge or a distinct source of valid knowledge but is still a distinct experience that must be distinguished from knowledge and given a separate name. "The experience which reveals the new (i.e. knowledge proper) is called anubhūti, whereas reproduced knowledge is called smṛti".[8]

But we can point out that memory too has novelty, i.e. anadhigatatva or a character which does not belong to the original apprehension and that feature is the pastness of its object. Memory is not mere photographic reproduction of a previous experience; it is not wholly and only identical with the content of the past experience. It apprehends the events and objects as qualified by the special attribute of 'being past', just as the events and objects of perception are apprehended as qualified by the attribute of 'being present'.

Madhvācārya goes even a step further and insists that memory is not merely not wholly dependent upon the earlier apprehension, but argues that it itself is a kind of direct apprehension. We will discuss this view later after dealing with all objections against memory. So far as the charge of the absence of anadhigatatva is concerned, we may say that in a sense (explained already) anadhigatatva does belong to memory also; but as a matter of fact it cannot be considered to be a very essential part of validity. Validity is constituted only by yāthārthya understood in its broad sense and as such memory-knowledge too, is valid.

There are some more objections of minor importance against validity of memory. Thus it is argued that a certain definition of valid knowledge does not include memory in its scope: valid knowledge is that which determines the objects without depending on other sources of knowledge;[9] since memory depends upon earlier perception, inference or testimony, it cannot be valid. The answer to such an objection is that there is practically no knowledge which does not depend upon any other source of knowledge. Inference depends upon earlier perception, inference etc. for the knowledge of vyapti; Upamāna depends upon the knowledge from testimony; testimony itself depends upon perception and understanding the meaning of words; the same is true of presumption, non-apprehension etc. Therefore it cannot be cited as a fault and at least not in the case of memory alone.

It cannot be held that smṛti cannot be valid because it has no useful purpose to serve; the reason is that utility cannot be a defining property of validity. Whether valid knowledge has utility or not is beside the point. Our knowledge that we are walking on grass does not serve any practical purpose but that does not make the knowledge invalid. It is also not correct to believe that memory has no practical purpose to serve. It reminds us of pleasant experiences and makes us seek them; it strengthens the potencies of impressions and organises the contents systematically; it evokes the feelings of love or hate; smṛti facilitates learning and arouses the sense of personal identity. Such and many other purposes are served by memory and yet we maintain that it is both valid and useful and do not maintain that it is valid because it is useful.

A critic cannot maintain that we can know the past by inference from the retention of the impressions of the past experience, or from the revival of the impressions; the reason is that such an inference itself would depend upon memory. Hence for knowing the past we need only a separate pramāṇa and that is memory.

Among the modern thinkers, we may refer to the arguments made by G.P. Das[10] against memory as a form of valid knowledge and also as a pramāṇa. These arguments are not entirely new and different from those we have already discussed.

He maintains that in one sense, memory is a necessary condition for the employment of the word cognition. In other words, according to him, we acquire various cognitions or knowledge-claims and different pramāṇas are nothing but different methods of justifying these knowledge-claims. They adduce grounds in support of our knowledge-claims. Only when the knowledge-claim is justified that it becomes proper knowledge. The process of justification is a process of having doubts and deliberations and of applying various concepts, of assimilating, classifying etc. Hence, saṁśaya (doubt), niścaya (deliberation), garva (laying a claim) and smaraṇa (remembrance) are a set of ideas which are necessarily linked up with the idea of knowledge. Thus in a method by which people adduce grounds for their knowledge-claims or by which they seek to establish their assertions of knowledge, memory is very important but only as a condition for the employment of the word cognition or knowledge claim. In this sense, idea of knowledge and idea of memory go together. In short, memory is a condition of knowledge but is not itself a cognition.

He further argues that in another sense, memory constitutes a form of cognition which cannot qualify as knowledge when we consider the distinctive character of knowledge. This distinctive character is nothing but what is given by the Advaitins as a cognition which is not internalised previously and which is not set aside (Anadhigata-abādhitārtha-viṣayaka-jñānatvam pramātvam।). In his own words, "to know is to know that something is thus and so. This is what we did not cognise before. If I cognised before, then I cannot be said to know it now. I am said to remember what I knew before. It is a piece of memory-cognition, not a piece of knowledge".

He uses a similie of membership in this context and says that knowledge is like membership. Renewal of membership is not new acquisition of membership. Hence, "I was happy" is a memory-cognition but not knowledge because it needs that I must have had knowledge about myself being happy already before.

He even maintains that cognitions like "I was sound asleep" or "I was dreaming" are not only not knowledges but they are not even memory-cognitions. The reason is that there is no earlier cognition (in fact it is impossible to have one) which can be expressed in the form, "I am sound asleep" or "I am dreaming", and which can be remembered afterwards in the form, "I was sound asleep", or "I was dreaming". They are what vedāntaparibhāṣā calls Iśvarasākṣīpratyakṣa or self-established direct knowledge.

The conclusion he arrives at is : ". . . . the point which I want to drive home is that the word 'memory' is used in at least two senses as our above discussion shows. In one sense, memory is one of the necessary conditions for the employment of the word 'cognition'. In another sense, memory constitutes a form of cognition which cannot qualify as knowledge".[11]

Analysing these views, we note that two senses of memory are not as distinct and exclusive as they are made out to be. Memory which serves as a necessary condition for the employment of the word 'cognition' is nothing but a process or a function of remembering involved in perception, inference, comparison, testimony etc. Moreover, it is not just any function, but an essentially cognitive function—its essence being cognising again an object, a word, a relation, an action etc. It is such an act of remembering that plays an auxiliary role in perception, inference etc. and if it were to result in invalid cognition, even the perceptual or inferential knowledge based upon it would be invalid. In this context, it may also be pointed out that pramāṇs are not merely the methods of justifying or supporting the knowledge claims, they are also the processes which generate the cognitions. The distinction which G.P. Das makes between 'sources of knowledge" (explaining the origin of knowledge) and 'methods of knowledge" (adducing grounds for our knowledge-claims) is artificial and has no basis in reality, and hence his insistence that methods of knowledge alone are pramāṇas is unacceptable.

Pramāṇas generate and also justify the knowledge-claims. Since this function is performed by memory also, there is no reason why memory cannot be a pramāṇa.

The other sense of memory — that it is a form of cognition (but which cannot qualify as knowledge)— need not be supposed to be entirely different from the sense already discussed. Remembering which is an essential condition in other knowledges is itself a cognitive process, i.e. a process which produces its own cognition. The question is : does this cognition qualify as knowledge or not ? The answer given by G.P. Das is that it does not, and let us examine the reason he has given for it. He refers to the anadhigatatva of knowledge which has been already examined threadbare. He considers this as a distinctive character of knowledge but we have already shown it to be irrelevant to the validity of knowledge. He argues that what we cognised before, we cannot be said to know now; we simply remember what we have cognised before.

It is true that in day-to-day life we say that we remember (and not that we know) when we are referring to past cognitions. But this is because in everyday life we are not very exact and particular about the employment of words. Many times when we say that we remember, what we mean is that we know through remembrance. Moreover, it is also true that what is not remembered even with a great effort is also admitted as having escaped from our knowledge, and we have no doubt in our mind that memory alone is an instrument which can restore it back to our knowledge. If knowledge by its very nature were to be devoid of memory (smṛtivyāvṛta), then pastness of an object would never be a datum of knowledge. The really distinctive character of knowledge is not anadhigatatva but yāthārthya and it belongs to memory.

The distinction which G.P. Das makes between two assertions, viz. "I was happy" and "I was dreaming" can be explained consistently with our viewpoint also. G.P. Das maintains that 'I was happy' is not direct knowledge but only memory-cognition which fails to qualify as knowledge because here we are simply remembering what we had cognised before. 'I was dreaming' is a direct knowledge of Iśvarasākṣīpratyakṣa variety; it is not memory-cognition as it does not depend upon any earlier cognition. We maintain that both are the instances of memory-cognitions which have a claim to knowledge. One is an instance of is an instance of representational memory at work which perceives the past through the contact provided by impressions; the other is an instance of presentational memory which has a direct perception of the past. Memory is both presentational-representational in nature.

Arguments favouring memory as pramā and pramāṇa :

Treating memory as purely representational has its problems. If we are aware of only impressions or images which are supposed to represent the past, a problem arises if this is a sufficient evidence for the past. The impressions are caused by the first experiences. But then the impressions relate only to the actual state of the events or objects as they were experienced. So if the impressions correspond to the objective content of experience, how do they produce the memory-knowledge of the pastness of the event or object?

Madhvācārya, while admitting the validity of memory, advocates a theory of memory which overcomes the above mentioned difficulty. According to him, the memory experiences are not just the reflections of impressions. They are direct apprehensions of the mind looking into the past. He brings memory under perception and treats it as a direct perception of the past by the mind. There are seven kinds of perceptual knowledges according to him—six being due to six sense organs and the seventh being the memory-knowledge obtained by the mind acting as the independent instrument of knowledge.[12]

The validity of this perceptual knowledge is not merely inferential, because in that case even the perception of an object will have to be treated as an inference from an effect to its cause (from the knowledge of the existent object to its existence). As in the case of other perceptual knowledge, even memory cognition is validated by intuition of sākṣī or sākṣipratyakṣa.

The contact or sannikarṣa necessary for this kind of perceptual knowledge is provided by the impressions (saṁskāras) left on the mind by the earlier direct apprehension. With the aid of these impressions, the mind can perceive the past and that mind has such a capacity to penetrate into the past and future is confirmed by the instances of extra- ordinary perceptions of yogis.

These are not treated as instances of inference. It is true that memory-cognition and yogic perceptions differ from each other in certain important respects. Memory is limited to the sphere of previously experienced objects or events which have left their impressions which in their turn act as connecting links with the past. (But still, memory-perceptions are not purely and simply the reflections or reproductions of impressions). The yogic perceptions of past and future have no such limitations as these are made possible by the saṁskāras or connecting links supplied by the power of yogic merit.

Insofar as memory-perception is uncontradicted and true (yathārtha), memory is fully entitled to the status of pramāṇa. In the words of Dr. B.N.K. Sharma,[13] "As a Realist Madhvā establishes the right to validity of memory and anuvāda, both in the enlarged sense of the term "Yāthārthyam", as defined by him and in the narrow sense of 'anadhigatārthagantṛ' accepted by the Bhāṭṭas and the Advaitins". In other words, memory perception gives us the knowledge of object as it actually was in a particular space-time setting and was actually perceived by the person according to the extent of his capacity; memory- perception also apprehends the object as not apprehended before, viz. in its pastness.

This, in essence is the substance of Madhvācārya's theory of memory. He also considers various other arguments supporting the claim of memory and objections to such a claim. Most of these are already considered in detail in the earlier section. His main contention is that memory ought to be recognised as a primary source of our knowledge concerning the past. This is a view which has been afterwards shared by many Indian as well as Western thinkers. All of them have insisted that in the absence of memory, we should never know that there was any past at all. If memory is treated as invalid, there would be no proof of our past experiences having occurred to us:

Pūrvānubhute kim mānamityukte syāt, kimuttaram?

(Madhvācārya's Anu-vyākhyāna; ii.1.4)[14]

This problem may not arise so long as we are referring to general remembrance regarding general events where even if all people lose their memory of events, the past can be still reconstructed with the help of written and other physical records which can be cross-checked or with the help of other scientific theories which support our contention. But the problem arises when we are referring to our own personal experience and its remembrance. If I lose my memory, I cannot reconstruct my past experience for myself. In this instance, the undisturbed memories of others will hardly have any binding force on me so far as I am concerned. Thus memory is extremely important in knowing the past. It is true that at times our memory-cognitions are invalid but then we also have erroneous perceptions and inferences. These do not affect the general validity of perception and inference. Why should memory alone be an exception?

Memory is therefore valid knowledge and a kind of perception of the past. A similar status to memory has also been assigned by the Western thinkers like Samuel Alexander, Thomas Reid, Bertrand Russell etc. According to Alexander, memory is an immediate perception of the pastness of an object, the object is directly present before our mind bearing on its face the mark of pastness. Even according to Reid memory is an original but unaccountable faculty like perception, and it is responsible for our immediate knowledge of things past. Memory as a source of knowledge is also responsible for the acquisition of the notion of duration, for the conviction of our own continued existence over a period of time and also for our notion of personal identity. Russell describes memory as the purest example of mirror-knowledge or knowledge of facts and comparable to sensation which is another source of knowledge of facts. As Russell puts it, "When I remember a piece of music or a friend's face, my state of mind resembles . . . what it was when I heard the music or saw the face".[15]

We note that there is a close resemblance between Madhvācārya's treatment of memory as a kind of perception and Russell's explanation of memory as a kind of mirror-knowledge comparable to perception. But their accounts have one more resemblance of considerable importance and it is in respect of the validity of memory-knowledge. As already mentioned, according to Madhvācārya, memory-knowledge is validated by Sākṣī who is the ultimate arbitrator of validity of any knowledge. Sākṣī judges upon the validity of knowledge; he is the intuitor of knowledge and also its validity. Sākṣi-pratyakṣa corresponds to the faculty of a priori cognitions and is individual to each person. Even for Russell, memory-statements form a kind of intuitive judgements—the judgements which are self-evident and trustworthy and for which no further reason can be given. They are not derived from certain other judgements. He admits that self-evidence and trustworthiness of memory are relative to the vividness of experience and to its nearness in time.

Even Jainas accept memory as a kind of valid knowledge and also as a means of valid knowledge. But it is a form of mediate knowledge according to them. Mediate knowledge is parokṣa-jñāna or non-perceptual knowledge which is definitive and authentic but lacks in immediacy and lucidity. Recollection is a knowledge which has for its condition the stimulation of an impression. Since it is conditioned by the stimulation of impression (and therefore not immediate) it is mediate knowledge. It is an organ of knowledge. Since it is never found to be discrepant with fact which is further attested by successful activity. Hemacandra, while admitting the status of memory as valid knowledge and an organ of valid knowledge considers the objection that memory has no objective basis (because it does not cognise a datum perceived at the present). His argument is that the reality of object and not its actually felt presence is the condition of the validity of a cognition. Revelation of the relevant object is a sufficient criterion and its is satisfied by memory. Just as light, generated by its own conditions reveals various objects, similarly, a cognition generated by its own conditions reveals its relevant object. Hemacandra also refers to the argument already discussed, viz. that based upon the mystic perception of the past and future objects (but not generated by the actually felt presence of an object) and the argument based upon the dependence of inference on memory.

The other school in Indian Philosophy which has acknowledged the important status of memory in the field of knowledge is viśiṣṭādvaita. It is true that the earlier Viśiṣṭādvaitic thinkers like Varada Nārāyaṇa Bhaṭṭāraka did not accept the validity of smṛti because smṛti is a knowledge of knowledge and does not present the corresponding object to the perceiver. More or less the same line of argument is also adopted by Viṣṇu-citta and Varada Viṣṇu Miśra. Nātha Muni and Parāśara Bhaṭṭāraka had expressed themselves in favour of smṛti.

Both Vedānta Deśika and Meghanādāri accept memory as a kind of valid knowledge. As for its status as a means of valid knowledge, Vedānta Deśika admits it as a mode of perception. Thus it is not a source of knowledge independent of perception, but is to be included within the pramāṇa which is responsible for it, i.e. perception. Even Meghānādari argues in favour of memory as a pramāṇa insisting that it is a spontaneous revelation of the remembered object and hence not dependent on any other pramāṇa.

In his Nyāya-Pariśudhi, Vedānta Deśika discusses various arguments favouring the status of memory as a valid knowledge and as an organ of knowledge. He summarises all important arguments and answers them one by one. He argues : Nanu smṛtirna pramāṇamavidyamānaviṣayatvāt, ananubhūtitvāt, bhramasaṁbhavācceti cenna, smṛtimātrāprāmaṇyasya prathamāhnike pratikṣiptatvat, abādhitabāhyārthadarśanāt, atītānāgataviṣayānumānā—anumānādi-bādhaprasaṅgāt, sarvalokavirodhāt, ananubhūte arthāntare'pi smṛtiprasaṅgāt, smṛterapi svaprakāśatve'pi vedyākāre saṁskārādisāpekṣatvāt |[16]

If it is argued that smṛti is not of the nature of valid knowledge because its object is not directly present, it is not of the nature of direct apprehension and that it is likely to be erroneous, we do not accept it for the following reasons —

Becasue the invalidity of entire memory as such is discarded in the first Ahnika itself (where pramā is defined as Yathāvasthitavyavahārānuguṇam jñānam); because the knowledge of its object is seen to be uncontradicted; because this will lead to the rejection of inference and other sources (like testimony, yogic perception etc.) which refer to past and future objects; because this contradicts the general belief and because smṛti too is capable of revealing its object of knowledge by itself. In fact with the disappearance of memory, even the earlier apprehension disappears. It cannot be held to be invalid because of its dependence (on other pramāṇas) or paratantratva; because this kind of paratantratva is found to be present everywhere. Moreover, smṛti is independent so far as the manifestation of its object is concerned and its ability to lead to successful action is concerned. (Svaviṣayaprakāśavyavahārayostu smṛterapi svatantratvāt ।) Memory cannot be held to be invalid because of its alleged inability to serve any practical purpose; because then even the direct apprehension of an insignificant object like a blade of grass would be invalid. Niṣprayojanatvādaprāmāṇyamiti cenna, tṛṇādiviṣayapratyakṣādinā'naikāntyāt ।[17] Smṛti fulfils various purposes in life. By smṛti alone we contemplate on the course of our every-day life; by smṛti alone the poets write poetry; it is due to smṛti that the use of inference and words is possible; and it is by smṛti alone that the parābhakti or the highest kind of devotion instrumental in the attainment of liberation is possible. (Smṛtyaiva hi jagatām kṛtakṛtapratyavekṣaṇādisiddhiḥ, smṛtyaiva hi kavayaḥ kāvyāni kavayanti । Smṛtyaiva hi śabdānumānayoḥ. pravṛttiḥ । parabhaktyādiniṣpattiśca ।[18]

It would be improper to say that all these are due to prior apprehension and not due to remembrance; because in that case it is better to hold the Divine Resolve (Brahamasaṁkalpa) to be the only means of valid knowledge.

Vedānta Deśika speaks of three divisions of memory according to the three causes which generate them. These three divisions are :

(i) Right memory (caused by valid apprehension)

(ii) Erroneous memory (caused by error)

(iii) Doubtful memory (caused by doubt)

Thus all memory is not invalid; one based upon valid apprehension itself is of three kinds for Vedānta Deśika — Pratyakṣa, Anumāna and Śabda. It is obvious that corresponding to these, there will be three remembrances as well. Or one may accept only three pramāṇas with the clear understanding that three smṛti-types are included in three anubhava- types. Thus generally speaking, Vedānta Deśika accepts memory as a mode of perception but admits that remembrance of inference and testimony too is possible.

A modern thinker like Ācārya Jwālā Prasāda accepts memory as an instrument of knowledge, another instrument being anubhava. The valid means of knowledge are only the forms of anubhava but not those of memory. But anubhava and memory are admitted as sharing so many common features that it is very difficult to make any difference between them. There does not seem to be any genuine reason for denying the status of pramāṇa to memory, when like anubhava, memory too is an instrument of grasping the nature of an object, is steadfast in our mind and can be corroborated by the evidence of others when valid, admits the same kinds involves the same fallacies and is involved in every kind of knowledge.

Arvinda Sharma in his article in Indian Philosophical Quarterly on the role of memory in Hindu epistemology discusses the status assigned to memory so far and also the reasons for which the status needs to be re-examined. One of the reasons, according to him is that memory is the only internal means of knowing whether we have slept or dreamt; it is the memory of the dream which enables us to distinguish between it and the waking state.

Many times we know a thing but forget it after a lapse of time. When we remember what was known in the past, then the knowledge that we had knowledge is a new knowledge. (In the language of traditional epistemology, pastness of the object constitutes the uncognisedness or anadhigatatva of knowledge.)

Leading to the achievement of some end is one of the criteria of validity according to the pragmatic thinkers. On many occasions when original apprehension had not led to any successful activity or to the achievement of any end, the corresponding remembrance, has this feature. Is it not valid then?

Sharma's arguments are not exactly novel. But he makes an important point when he refers to three states of consciousness, waking, dreaming and deep sleep and to the fact that the distinction between the first two is cognised through memory alone. Similarly, the knowledge of sleeping or dreaming is also obtained through memory. The suggestion is that in these matters not only is smṛti a pramāṇa but it is the only pramāna.

The most important consideration in favour of memory being recognised as valid knowledge is that, whatever the counterarguments of the scholars, memory is accepted as valid knowledge in normal life. It is our own immediate and absolutely certain experience and various knowledges are obtained only through memory-experience. There is no other way of establishing the validity of any knowledge or its source except on the basis of universal human experience : Na hyasti pratyakṣādiprāmāṇyasādhakamanyallokavyavahārāt |[19]

The fact that Akṣapāda, Kaṇāda and others have not accepted memory as valid knowledge is no argument against it. Vedic texts do recognise that smṛti also is a source of knowledge :

(Vede mānaissahoktā smṛtirapi |[20]) There is a strong foundation for the validity of memory in the well-known statement from an unidentified scriptural text which enumerates memory among oher forms of valid knowledge : Smṛtiḥ pratyakṣamaitihyamanumānacatuṣṭayam pramāṇamiti vijñeyam dharmādyarthe mumukṣubhiḥ |[21]

Those desirous of liberation should, for the purpose of determining right course of action etc., understand by pramana these four things, viz. smṛti (memory), pratyakṣa (perception), aitihya (tradition) and anumāna (inference).

It is obvious that right from the vedic times upto the modern times, there have been critics and admirers of memory as a pramā and a pramāṇa. Various arguments and counter- arguments have been made in this context and these have been explained and examined so far. The problem to be considered now is what is the final outcome when we weigh these arguments and counter-arguments for their respective strength. The discussion of this problem is the subject-matter of the last section which follows.

References

1. The Khaṇḍanakhaṇḍakhādya of Shri Harsha—Translated by Ganganath Jha, Vol. I, p. 82.
2. Nyāya Mañjarī of Jayanta Bhaṭṭa, I — 21.
3. Ibid.
4. Praśastapādabhāṣya, edited by Pt. Durgadhar Jha, p. 628.
5. Nyāya-Sudhā of Jayatīrtha, p. 60.
6. Ibid, p. 61.
7. Sthāyitvenābhimatākāśādeḥ pūrvairavagatatvasaṁbhavāt tadviṣayānumānāderaprāmāṇyaprasaṅgat I - Meghanādāris Naya-dyu-maṇi quoted by S.N.Dasgupta, A History of Indian Philosophy, Vol.III, p. 215.
8. D.M.Datta, Six ways of knowing, p. 23.
9. Tatrānyapramāṇānapekṣamarthaparicchedakam jñānam pramāṇam-
   Meghanādāri in Naya-dyu-maṇi quoted by S.N.Dasgupta, History of Indian Philosophy, Vol. III, p. 239.
10. "Discussion on Arvind Sharma's article on 'The Role of Memory.......". - by G.P.Das, Indian Philosophical Quarterly, Vol. XI, No.1 January 1984, pp. 131 to 135.
11. Ibid, p. 135.
12. Pratyakṣam saptavidham, Sākṣiṣaḍindriyabhedena; manasapratyakṣajā smṛtiḥ I -
    Madhva in Pramāṇa-lakṣaṇa-quoted by B.N.K.Sharma, Philosophy of Madhvacarya, p. 139.
13. Ibid, p. 144.
14. Ibid, p. 140.
15. Human knowledge - its scope and limits, p. 440.
16. Nyāya-Pariśuddhi in Shreemadvedāntadeśikagranthamālā, edited by Aṇṇaṅgarācārya, p. 171.
17. Ibid, p. 171.
18. Ibid, p. 172.
19. Nyāya-Sudhā of Jayatirtha, p. 61.
20. Tattva-Muktā-Kalpa, IV, p. 125 .
21. Quoted by S.N.Dasgupta, A History of Indian Philosophy, Vol. IV, p. 165.

Conclusion

'I am a part of all that I have met;
Yet all experience is an arch whero
Gleams that untravell'd world,
whose margin fades,
For ever and for ever when I move'.

(Tennyson's Ulysses)

Human existence is a multifaceted phenomenon and human knowledge is one of its important facets. Indeed, as Tennyson says the possibilities of knowledge are endless like horizon. There is no limit to how much we can know and how we can know. The facts of knowledge and its exension are indisputable and generally taken for granted. The process of knowledge is very complicated and involves a number of factors. The stimuli keep on invading our senses and our rational faculty incessantly. At times we seem to receive meekly what is presented to us by our senses; these sensations are worked into perceptions, these into images, conceptions, ideas and all these into remembrances. In matters of perceptions, images, conceptions etc. we are intellectually active.

It is a prerogative of human beings to try to know about knowledge itself though it is a universal instinct to be curious and to try to know the world. While trying to know about knowledge, we ask various questions : what is the nature of knowledge, what is the relation between the knower, the known and the knowledge, when is the knowledge valid, what are the process responsible for producing valid knowledge etc.

In their attempt to answer these questions, human beings may discover processes which are not so very obvious like sense-experience and reasoning but they may also overlook those which are all too familiar. Familiarity does not merely breed contempt, it may also breed neglect.

Memory has met the latter fate in the hands of the learned. It is a universal occurrence. It is present in all processes leading to knowledge-even sense, experience is no exception. It itself is an independent experience producing its unique knowledge for which no other means are available. Thus the contribution of memory to knowledge is quite considerable and important. Still some philosophers are critical of the status of memory. The sceptics in the West argue that the evidence for memory-knowledge is far too short to justify its validity. Simply because we remember the past events, there is no guarantee that our belief in the past is justified. Now, it is a wellknown fact that scepticism in this narrow sense as the total denial of all knowledge so defines knowledge and specialy the requirements for claiming the knowledge that it makes all knowledge impossible. But if we understand knowledge in its broad (though perhaps 'weak') sense to mean the awareness of and belief in an object for which we have reasonably good evidence, there is no reason why memory- knowledge should be impossible.

Even scepticism can be understood in its broader meaning as an attitude of suspending judgement until critical analysis is complete. Thus, it is an attitude oil questioning any assumption until it can be subjected to rigorous examination. With this stimulating attitude of cautions philosophical reflection, we have examined various arguments made against memory as a kind of valid knowledge. The main argument against memory is derived from the notion of validity. The problem of validity is one of the most important problems in Indian Philosophy. Various accounts of validity are given and an attempt is made to show that these cannot be satisfied by memory. We have already examined these arguments in detail and concluded that either these are unimportant for the notion of validity or else these can be satisfied by memory also. Whether we consider faithful revelation of its object or novelty or fruitfulness or being of the nature of apprehension or independence from other pramāṇas, there is no important connotation of validity that does not belong to memory.

Many times these different notions of validity supplement each other and do not contradict each other. If valid knowledge is of the nature of direct apprehension which has immediacy, spontaneity, ability to cognise what was unknown before and to give rise to practically useful or fruitful activity, then all these features belong to memory as well. We accept then that validity means faithfulness of the knowledge to its object-content. Validity, in this sense belongs to memory and like the validity of any other knowledge, it can be confirmed by its steadiness, its consistency with the knowledge of others, and by its usefulness and practical consequences. We can thus combine various essential elements from different accounts of validity to form a broad concept of validity which belongs to memory-knowledge.

Along with these arguments, what should count as equally important is the common man's unwavering faith in the validity of his memory. We have innumerable instances of memory-knowledge which is absolutely certain and no man in his wits really questions whether what he remembers really happened or not.

In fact it is very difficult to deny validity to memory which so obviously belongs to it. Even thinkers like Vācaspati Miśra seem to admit it indirectly. In commenting on the definition of pramāṇa in the sūtra : upalabdhihetuḥ pramāṇam : Vācaspati Miśra first qualifies the term upalabdhi by the adjunct of being correct-yathārtha' to avoid the inclusion of doubt in pramāṇa. But since the new definition, viz. yathārthopalabdhiḥ pramāṇam would include memory also, he immediately states that all correct knowledges as such are not induced in pramāṇa but only those of the nature of direct apprehension. It means then that memory is correct knowledge according to him.

It is doubtless true that old man's memory or child's memory or a sick person's memory is not dependable. The memory-reports of even normal persons are at times distorted. But it is a secondary matter to decide the merits (guṇas) and defects (doṣas) which can determine or vitiate the accuracy of our memory. Primarily memory must be accepted as valid.

Fallacies are committed even in inference; perception is also vitiated by adverse external conditions like insufficiency of light, distance between the object and perceiver, minuteness of object, presence of distracting stimuli etc. and internal conditions like defects of sense organs, ill health etc. Words may give faulty knowledge through the shortcomings in our own understanding or because the authority is not in reality so. There is no reason why memory alone should be singled out and permanently debarred from the field of valid knowledge. Russell points out that in reality the fallacies of memory are not instances of memory at all.

Memory, admittedly then is valid knowledge; but the question of its status has another aspect too which has already been discussed threadbare in the chapter on 'status of memory'. This aspect pertains to the question : Is memory a source of knowledge?

Its role as an element in every source of knowledge is undeniably important; in its own right, it is valid knowledge too. But still it may be denied the status of pramāṇa or a source of knowledge. But it we assert memory-knowledge as valid and also the role of memory as a verificative instrument in every source of cognition, it is very odd to deny it the status of a source of knowledge. It is like admitting the importance of sense- experience in verifying empirical hypotheses but denying it the status of an independent source of knowledge.

Memory must be accepted as a source of knowledge because memory- knowledge which is pramā cannot be obtained through any other source. Our knowledge of the events from our own past, of our own identity, of the concept of duration and to some extent even of future, of causal connections are all derived from memory. Moreover, memory is independent in the manifestation of its own objects. It manifests its objects spontaneously. It may operate directly or through the images. Even when images are there, they are marked by their abstract and general nature and rarely if at all, they are individual and concrete in nature. Memory, thus, is not at all exact duplication of original experience. It is an independent experience capable of giving us valid knowledge of the object in its pastness. Many times, features of different experiences of the same object fuse together to give one composite memory-knowledge. The mistake of the Advaita idcalists is that they give an ontological explanation of the epistemological problem when they say that in the knowledge-process the subject-consciousness identifies itself with the object-consciousness and then naturally treat memory as a kind of dream-experience (as its object is not present) rather than a knowledge-experience.

Memory is a source of knowledge and a kind of perception of a distinctive type. In it, mind acts as a sense-organ and through the contact provided by the impressions perceives the object in its pastness. Just as the external perception reveals the present object spontaneously and immediately, memory reveals its own object, i.e. the object in its pastness in the same manner. The ultimate judge of validity in both the instances is Sākṣī.

It may be asked : How can a present memory take hold of its object as it originally was, because the object referred to by a certain act of memory has undergone many changes and has possibly ceased to exist in the interval in its former state? The answer is that just as the external sense organs are operative only in the present and perform the act of recognition through the help of the impressions, so also the mind, with the help of impressions perceives the object which has changed its previous state. Saṁskārasahakṛtam mano'nanubhūtāmapinivṛttapūrvāvasthām viṣayīkurvatsmaraṇam janayati। Yathāsaṁskārasahakṛtani So'yamityatītavatamānatvaviśiṣṭavaviṣayapratyabhijñāsādhanāni prākṛtendriyāṇi manovṛttim jñānam janayanti।[1].

A similar status to memory has been assigned by Vedānta-Deśika and also by modern Western philosophers and psychologists. The psychologists maintain that both perception and memory are private and immediate to the individual. Just as 'I see' is a sufficient evidence for justifying our perceptual knowledge, similarly 'I remember' is a sufficient evidence for our memory-knowledge. Like sensation, we cannot explain how memory operates. Even for describing recollected events, we use the same terms as used for describing the perceived events. It is indeed difficult to suggest the criteria that can distinguish perceptions from recollections.

For Russell also both memory-judgements and judgements of sensation are intuitive or-self evident; both are mirror-knowledges or knowledges of facts, both have immediacy.

Hence memorý is a way of knowing about the past just as sense-experience is a way of knowing about the present.

Samuel Alexandeı too accepts the immediate perception of the pastness of an object as a fact. Moreover, just as a single percept is full of movement towards other aspects of the thing perceived, even a single memory throws out feelers to other memories. A single percept and a single memory are both incomplete.

There are then, innumerable suggestions and corroborating evidences to the effect that memory is a distinct kind of perception and hence a source of valid knowledge. Though connected with the earlier experience, it has a distinct advantage in so far as the long-term memory has limitless possibilities of extending our knowledge of the past. To deny the status of pramā and pramāṇa to memory is to deny ourselves the chance of knowing our own past, our own identity, our own world and the Maker of this world and also of obtaining means for realising Him. It is like turning our back to the past and shutting our eyes to the future. They say, with the increase in knowledge, the knower also grows. Who would opt to be an intellectual dwarf by denying such an important avenue to knowledge like memory?

References

1. Jayatīrtha in Pramāṇapaddhati as quoted by D.N. Shanbhag in 'Some Problems in Dvaita Philosophy — in their dialectical setting, p. 66.

Appendix 'A'

Morgan and King on 'Memory'

Morgan and King speak of memory-store model involving short-term store and long-term store originally proposed by Atkinson and Shiffrin. In this model, the input is first held in sensory memory for a very brief time, then it passes along to private memory or a short-term store. In this store, major part of information processing occurs. If the material is adequately rehearsed, it passes into long-term store or secondary memory. Here, the information is placed into organized categories, and it resides virtually permanently. When we remember something, information is withdrawn, or retrived from the long-term store and put back into the working memory of short-term store for further processing. After that the information may be put back into the long- term store, or it may result in a response.

This model of memory fits pretty well with our subjective impressions when we are trying to remember something. Rehearsal is usually required to transfer short-term memory to long-term storage. We have the impression of having to search through the storage while remembering something. It is there and with some effort we can get it and get it right.

The phenomenon worth noting in this model is sensory memory or sensory register. The sensory channels can store a good deal of information for a brief time. Extensive experiments on visual and auditory channels are performed and they have given us impressive and objective information about human cognitive activity.

Short-term store has a very limited capacity. As already stated, rehearsals are necessary for converting short-term memory into long-term storage. Any disturbance in rehearsals results in the loss of information.

Long-term memory has almost unlimited capacity. The information is relatively permanently stored here. The problem of forgetting is a problem of retrieving from the storage. Another feature of this kind of memory is its organization. The information is not stored at random. Better organization leads to better memory. The information is remembered more quickly and more accurately because it is categorised.

Appendix 'B'

John Locke on 'Brutes have memory'

Locke, who was a widely travelled philosopher and a keen observer of nature notes in the tenth section of his chapter, 'Of Retention'[1] that several other animals (than humans) also have to a great degree the faculty of laying up and retaining the ideas that are brought into the mind. As he himself puts it, "For to pass by other instances, birds' learning of tunes, and the endeavours one may observe in them to hit the notes right, put it past doubt with me that they have perception, and retain ideas in their memories, and use them for patterns". The very fact that the birds try to conform their voices to notes confirms that they have already had the ideas of notes and have retained them. It may be admitted that imitation of notes mechanically serves the purpose of the bird's preservation. But on many occasions such a conformity with the notes of a foreign sound is of no use to the bird's preservation. Moreover, it will not at all be rational to suppose that birds, without sense and memory, can approach their notes, nearer by degrees, to a tune played yesterday; because if they do not have the idea of such a tune in their memory, now it exists nowhere and therefore birds do not have a pattern which they can imitate.

Appendix C

Olfactory sensation and memory [2]

Ages back, when we were quadrupeds, we used to make as much use of smell as of vision and hearing. As we became bipeds, our reliance upon smell became diminished. According to Michael Shipley, in the beginning, the brains of some of the animals were intimately connected with their universe of smells; but slowly the brain was covered with the 'thinking' grey matter and on the whole, the part of the brain connected with smell started getting under-utilised. But a large part of our brain is still connected with smell and similar cognition.

Even today the world of quadruped animals is more aware of smell than the human world and depends upon smell and its memory for its knowledge of the world. The young ones of rats and cats, who are visionless for a long time after their birth depend upon their sense of smell for identifying their mothers; cats frequently rub themselves against our body and leave behind a smelling mark before moving about. Deer, stags, leopards, tigers and the like animals make use of smell for the fundamental and the extremely important things of life. They mark out their exclusive territory with the uric smell, select the suitable mate with the help of smell, earn their food or beast of prey through smell and also identify their young ones with the aid of smell alone. It will not be an exaggeration to say that among all animals, dog excels in his capacity to know through smell. No other animal can surpass dog in his ability to pick up even a faint smell, to retain it in memory for a great length of time and to remember it on a suitable occasion. It is a common knowledge that just with the help of trail of smell, a dog can help find out thieves or run-away prisoners. But it is reported that a gas-leakage at about twelve feet under the ground which could not be detected even by very sensitive modern instruments could be identified by a dog.

In order to get more insight into the smell-related knowledge including remembrance, the National Geographic Institute and Philadelphia-based 'MONEL' Institute decided to jointly launch a research programme. One of its important findings is that smell can awaken memories; a person finds that he can experience again the incident associated with the smell. In fact the smells can serve as very powerful excitants of memories and stronger the smell, more powerful it is as an excitant; this power belongs to both the fair and the foul smell.

The discussion of the relation between olfactory sensation and memory reveals that there is a continuity between the animal world and human world in so far as both cognition and remembrance are concerned. It also confirms that like vision, even smell is intimately connected with memory. In fact, major part of the memory- knowledge of animals is through smell.

References

1. Essay concerning Human understanding - by John Locke - Chapter X, p. 84.
2 Athā to Gandhajijñāsā by Dr. C. Sahasrabuddhe, Maharashtra Times.

Bibliography

English Books

Alexander Samuel — 'Space, Time and Deity' published by MacMillan and Co. Ltd., London, 1920.

Ayer A.J. — 'The Problem of Knowledge' published by Penguine Books, New York, 1956.

Banerjee Nikunja Vihari — 'The Spirit of Indian Epistemology' — published by Arnold Heinemann Publishers (India) Ltd., New Delhi, 1974.

Bijalwan C.D. — 'Indian Theory of Knowledge' based upon Jayanta's Nyāyanañjari published by Heritage Publishers, New Delhi, 1977.

Boring, Langfeld and Weld — 'Foundations of Psychology' — published by John Wiley and Sons Inc., New York, 1948.

Chatterjee S.C. — 'The Nyaya Theory of Knowledge' published by University of Calcutta, 1950.

Chatterjee S.C. — 'The Problems of Philosophy' published by University of Calcutta, 1964.

Dasgupta Surendranth — 'A History of Indian Philosophy', Vol 3 and 4, published by Cambridge University Press, London, 1952, 1961 respectively.

Datta D.M. — 'The Six Ways of Knowing' published by University of Calcutta, 1972.

Gopalan S. — 'Outlines of Jainism' published by Wiley Eastern Ltd., New Delhi, 1975.

James William - 'The Principles of Psychology' Dover Publications Inc., U.S.A., 1890.

Jwala Prasad — 'History of Indian Epistemology' published by Munshiram Manoharlal, Delhi, 1958.

Locke John — 'Essay Concering Human Understanding' edited by A. Seth Pringle-Pattison, published by Oxford Clarendon Press, Oxford, 1924.

Matilal Bimal Krishna — 'Perception — An Essay on Classical Indian Theories of Error' published by Clarendon Press, Oxford, 1986.

Mehta Mohan Lal — 'Jaina Philosophy' published by Vidyāśrama Research Institute, Varanasi, 1971.

Mohanty Jitendranath — 'Gangeśa's Theory of Truth' published by Centre of Advanced Study in Philosophy, Śāntiniketana, West Bengal, 1966.

Mookerjee Satkari and Tatia Nathmal — 'A Critique of Organ of Knowledge' (based on Hemacandra's Pramāṇa-Mīmāṁsā), published by Bharati Jaina Parishat, Calcutta, 1946.

Morgan C.T. and King R.A. — 'Introduction to Psychology' published by Tata-MacGraw Hill Publishing Company 1975 (fifth edition).

Munn Norman L. — 'The Fundamentals of Human Adjustment' published by George G. Harrap & Co. Ltd., London, 1961.

Ramachandran T.R. — 'Ḍvaita Vedanta' published by Arnold Heinemann Publishers (India) Pvt. Ltd., Delhi, 1976.

Reid Thomas — 'Essays on the Intellectual Powers of Man' edited and abridged by A.D. Woozley, published by MacMillan & Co. Ltd., London, 1941.

Russell Bertrand — 'The Analysis of Mind' published by George Allen and Unwin Ltd., London, 1921

Russell Bertrand — 'The Problems of Philosophy' published by Oxford University Press, 1943.

Russell Bertrand — 'Human Knowledge : Its Scope and Limits' published by George Allen and Unwin Ltd., London, 1948.

Shanbhag D.N. — 'Some Problems in Dvaita Philosophy in Their Dialectical Settings' published by Shri Rama Prakashana, Dharwad, 1980.

Sharma B.N.K. — 'Philosophy of Śrī Madhvācārya' (first edition), published by Bharatiya Vidya Bhavan, Bombay, 1962.

Sharma B.N.K. — 'Philosokphy of Śrī Madhvācārya' (Revised edition), published by Motilal Banarsidas, New Delhi, 1986.

Singh Satyavrata — 'Vedānta Deśika — His Life, Works and Philosophy' published by Chowkhamba Sanskrit Series, Varanasi, 1958.

Sinha Jadunath — 'Indian Psychology', Vol. I (Cognition), published by Sinha Publishing House, Calcutta, 1958.

Sinha Jadunath — 'A History of Indian Philosophy (Vol. III)' published by Sinha Publishing House, Calcutta, 1971.

Srīnivāsachari P.N. — 'The Philosophy of Viśiṣṭādvaita' published by Adyar Library and Research Centre, Madras, 1943.

Stout G.F. — ' A Manual of Psychology' published by University Tutorial Press, London, 1913.

Stout G.F. — 'Studies in Philosophy and Psychology' published by MachMillan & co. Ltd., London, 1930.

Sundaram P.K. — 'Advaita Epistemology with Special Reference to Iṣṭasiddhi' published by University of Madras, 1968.

Titchner Edward Bradford — 'A Beginner's Psychology' published by The MacMillan Co., New York, 1923.

Varadachari K.C. — 'Śrī Rāmānuja's Theory of Knowledge — A Study' published by Tirumalai-Tirupati Devasthanam's Press, Tirupati, 1956.

Vidyarthi P.B. — 'Knowledge, Self and God in Rāmānuja' published by Oriental Publishers and Distributors, New Delhi, 1978.

Sanskṛta Books

Bhagavadgītā — by Dr. S. Radhakrishnan, published by George Allen and Unwin Ltd., London, 1948.

Khaṇḍanakhaṇḍakhādya — by Śrī Harṣa, Translated by Ganganath Jha; Vol. I, Second edition; Shri Satguru Publications, Delhi, 1986.

Nyāya Mañjarī — by Jayanṭha Bhaṭṭa, edited by Pandit Śrī Sūrya Nārāyaṇa Śukla, published by Jay Kṛṣṇadāsa Haridāsa Gupta; The Chowkhamba Sanskrit Series Office, Benares, 1936.

Nyāya-Pariśuddhi-(in Śrīmaḍ Vedāntadeśika Granthamālā) — by Vedāntadeśika, edited by Śrī Kāñci - Prativādibhayaṁkara Aṇṇaṅgarācāry, published by Granthamala Office, 39, Sannidhi Street; Conjeeveram, 1940.

Nyāya-sudhā — by Jayatīrtha, published by Motilal Banarasidas.

Praśastapādaabhāṣya — by Praśastapāda — with Nyāyakandali of Śrīdhara; edited by Vindhyeśvarīprasāda Dvivedin, Vol. IV, published by Lazarus & Co., Benares, 1895.

Praśastapādabhāṣya — by Praśastapāda, edited by Durgādhara Jha, published by Sampurnananda Sanskrta Visvavidyalaya, Varanasi, 1977.

Tarka Bhāṣā — by Keśava Miśra, edited by A.B. Gajendragadkar and R.D. Karmarkar, published by R.D. Karmarkar, S.P. College, Pune, 1934.

Tarka-Saṁgraha — by Annam Bhaṭṭa, edited by Y.V. Athalye and M.R. Bodas, published by Bhandarkar Oriental Research Institute, Pune 1974 (second edition).

Vedanta Paribhāṣā — by Dharmarāja Adhvarin, edited by S.S. Suryanarayana Sastri, published by Adyar Library, Madras, 1942.

Yatīndramatadīpikā — by Śrīnivāsadāsa, published by Sri Ramakrishna Math, Madras, 1949.

Marathi Books

Bhāratiya Saṁskṛtikośa, Vol. X, Bharatiya Samskṛtikoṣa Maṇḍala Prakāśana, Pune, 1979.

Bhāratīya Mānasaśāstra athavā sārtha aṇi savivaraṇa Pātañjala-Yoga-Darśana- Kṛṣṇājī Keśava Kolhaṭakarakṛta, Dhavale Prakaśana; Shaka 1873.

Śrī Tukāramamahārajānci Sārtha Gāthā, Editor—Ha. bha-pa.sa-ke.

Neurgaonkar — Prācārya Dandekar Dhārmika va Sāṁskṛtika Vāṅmaya Prakāśana Maṇḍala, Pune, 1978.

Encyclopedia, Journals etc.

The Encyclopaedia of Philosophy, Vol. 3, 5, 6, published by the MacMillan Company and the Free Press, New York, U.S.A., 1967.

Indian Philosophical Quarterly, Vol. X, No. 4, July, 1983, published by University of Poona, Pune. Name of the Article — The Role of Memory in Hindu Epistemology and Its Religious Implications by Prof. Arvind Sharma.

Indian Philosophical Quarterly, Vol. XI, No. 1 January, 1984; published by University of Poona. Discussion on the article by Prof. Arvind Sharma — by G.P. Das.

Indian Philosophical Quarterly — Vol. XII, No. 2, April-June 1985, published by University of Poona, Pune. Article, on 'Hume's Concept of Memory' by Sukla Parai.

Research Paper on Dvaita Epistemology by Dr. S.G. Mudgal.

Article in Maharashtra Times — page 9; Science Supplement; Wednesday, 14th December, 1988; Athā'to Gandhajijñāsā by Dr. Chandrakanta Sahastrabuddhe.

Śrī Tukārāmāñcī Nāmāvalī Sārtha Gāthā, editor—Pra. bhā pā Sa-kea

Neurasonkar — Prācārya Dāṇḍekar Dhārmika va Saṁskṛti Vāṅmaya Prakāśana Maṇḍala Pune 1978

Encyclopedias Journals etc

The Encyclopaedia of Philosophy, Vol. 3, 5, 6, published by the MacMillan Company and the Free Press, New York, U.S.A., 1967.

Indian Philosophical Quarterly, Vol. X, No. 4, July, 1983, published by University of Poona, Pune. Name of the Article — The Role of Memory in Hindu Epistemology and its Religious implications by Prof. Arvind Sharma.

Indian Philosophical Quarterly, Vol. XI, No. 1 January, 1984 published by University of Poona. Discussion on the article by Prof. Arvind Sharma — by G.P. Das.

Indian Philosophical Quarterly — Vol. XII, No. 2, April-June 1985, published by University of Poona, Pune. Article on Hume's Concept of Memory by Sukla Parat.

Research Paper on Dvaita Epistemology by Dr. S.G. Mudgal.

Article in Mahārāshtra Times — page 9, Science Supplement Wednesday, 7th December, 1988. Atha Gandhajijñāsā by Dr. Chandrakānta Sahasrabuddhe.

INDEX